The Absolute Beginner's Memory Reference Card

Different Kinds of Memory

Conventional Memory
Conventional memory is the first 640K of RAM on your system. DOS uses conventional memory to load all your software programs—as well as some basic DOS files.

Upper Memory
Upper memory is the area of RAM between 640K and 1M. DOS uses upper memory to store various BIOS routines, as well as video memory. Because DOS doesn't use all of the upper memory area, there are numerous upper memory blocks that can be used (in DOS 5 or later) to load device drivers and other small programs.

High Memory
The high memory area is the first 64K RAM of extended memory.

Extended Memory
Extended memory is any RAM above the 1M mark.

Expanded Memory
Expanded memory is RAM linked through a special page frame in upper memory to available memory above 1M. Expanded memory was originally used to take advantage of memory above 1M before DOS could access this memory; with the advent of extended memory, expanded memory is infrequently used.

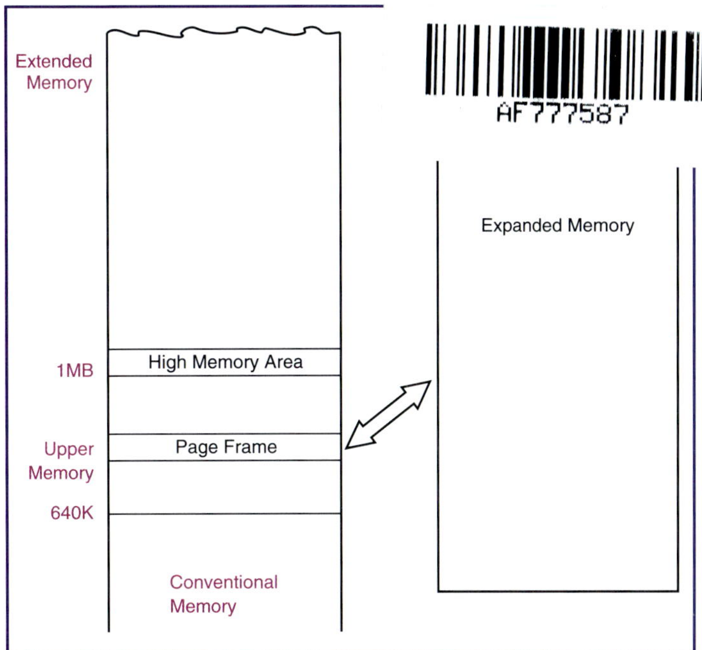

Different kinds of memory.

Bits and Bytes

UNIT	SIZE
byte	8 bits
kilobyte	1,024 bytes
megabyte	1,048,576 bytes
gigabyte	1,073,741,824 bytes

The Difference Between Memory and Disk Storage

	MEMORY	DISKS
Usage	Temporary storage	Permanent storage
Speed	Fast	Slow
Amount of Storage Space	Small	Large
Storage Method	Electronic	Physical

The Difference between RAM and ROM

	RAM	ROM
Read capability	Yes	Yes
Write capability	Yes	No
Volatile	Yes	No
Speed	Slower	Faster
Storage type	Temporary	Permanent
Ideal for storing:	Data that changes frequently	Data that doesn't change

DOS Memory Management Commands

`CHKDSK`	The `CHKDSK` command, typed at the DOS prompt, checks the status of a disk and displays information about your system's use of conventional memory.
`DEVICE`	The `DEVICE` command, located in the CONFIG.SYS file, is used to load device drivers into memory.
`DEVICEHIGH`	The `DEVICEHIGH` command, located in the CONFIG.SYS file, is identical to the `DEVICE` command, except that it loads the device driver into your system's upper memory area.
`DOS`	The `DOS` command, located in the CONFIG.SYS file, is used to load DOS into the high memory area (HMA) and/or create upper memory blocks (UMBs).
EMM386.EXE	The EMM386.EXE driver provides access to the upper memory area and uses extended memory to simulate expanded memory. This driver must be loaded by a `DEVICE` command in your CONFIG.SYS file.
HIMEM.SYS	The HIMEM.SYS driver is an extended memory manager and provides access to your PC's high memory area (HMA). This driver must be loaded by a `DEVICE` command in your CONFIG.SYS file.
`LOADHIGH`	The `LOADHIGH` command, located in the AUTOEXEC.BAT file, is used to load device drivers and programs into your system's upper memory area.
`MEM`	The `MEM` command, typed at the DOS prompt, displays details of your system's memory use.
MEMMAKER	MEMMAKER is a DOS 6 utility program that optimizes your system's use of memory. It automatically edits your CONFIG.SYS and AUTOEXEC.BAT files to move device drivers and programs to upper memory in the most efficient manner.
RAMDRIVE.SYS	The RAMDRIVE.SYS driver is used to create a RAM disk using your system's memory. This driver must be loaded by a `DEVICE` command in your CONFIG.SYS file.
SMARTDRV.EXE	The SMARTDRV.EXE driver is used to create a disk cache using your system's memory. This driver must be loaded in your AUTOEXEC.BAT file.

Types of Memory Chips

DIP *Dual in-line package.* This chip is a flat rectangle with 16 metal legs, and it kind of looks like a spider. DIPs plug into little sockets on your motherboard.

SIMM *Single in-line memory module.* A SIMM is kind of like a miniature expansion card, a few inches long, that has nine RAM chips presoldered to the card. A SIMM doesn't have legs (it has an edge connector instead) and slides into a SIMM socket on your motherboard.

SIP *Single in-line package.* A SIP is a long, multichip chip, kind of like a SIMM. The big difference between a SIMM and a SIP is that a SIP has a single row of legs instead of an edge connector.

ZIP *Zigzag in-line package.* A ZIP is a SIP with two rows of legs, staggered on the same edge of the chip.

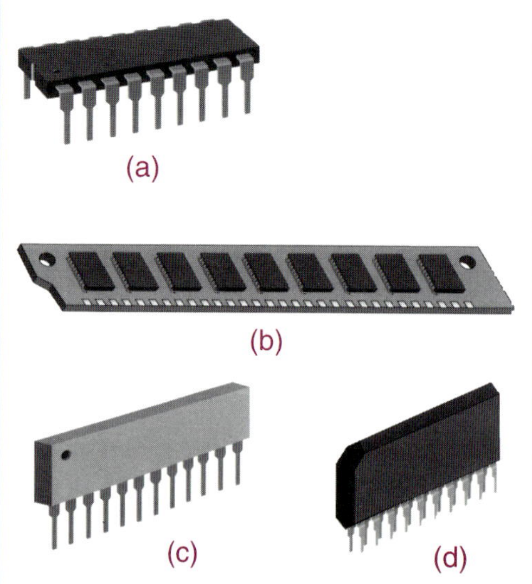

Examples of a DIP (a), a SIMM (b), a SIP (c), and a ZIP (d) chip.

Absolute Beginner's Guide to Memory Management

Absolute Beginner's Guide to Memory Management

Mike Miller

SAMS PUBLISHING

A Division of Prentice Hall Computer Publishing
11711 North College, Carmel, Indiana 46032 USA

FIRST EDITION

International Standard Book Number: 0-672-30282-9

Library of Congress Catalog Card Number: 92-82092

96 95 94 93 4 3 2 1

Interpretation of the printing code: the rightmost double-digit number is the year of the book's printing; the rightmost single-digit, the number of the book's printing. For example, a printing code of 93-1 shows that the first printing of the book occurred in 1993.

Composed in MCPdigital by Prentice Hall Computer Publishing

Printed in the United States of America

Trademarks

Publisher
Richard K. Swadley

Acquisitions Manager
Jordan Gold

Acquisitions Editor
Gregg Bushyeager

Development Editor
Mark Taber

Senior Editor
Grant Fairchild

Editorial Coordinator
Rebecca S. Freeman

Editorial Assistant
Sharon Cox

Formatter
Bill Whitmer

Technical Reviewer
James P. McCarter

Marketing Manager
Greg Wiegand

Director of Production and Manufacturing
Jeff Valler

Production Manager
Corinne Walls

Imprint Manager
Kelli Widdifield

Book Designer
Michele Laseau

Production Analyst
Mary Beth Wakefield

Proofreading/Indexing Coordinator
Joelynn Gifford

Graphics Image Specialists
Dennis Sheehan
Susan VandeWalle

Production
Christine Cook
Lisa Daughtery
Mitzi Gianakos
Howard Jones
John Kane
Angela Pozodol
Linda Quigley
Barbara Webster
Alyssa Yesh

Indexer
Johnna Van Hoose

Overview

Part II Managing Your System's Memory

Part III Easy Memory Setups Anyone Can Do

Appendices

CONTENTS

Appendices

Acknowledgments

Thanks to Gregg Bushyeager, Mark Taber, Richard Swadley, and the whole Sams team for a very enjoyable experience.

About the Author

Mike Miller is Director of Marketing Strategies for Prentice Hall Computer Publishing and the author of numerous books, including the best-selling *OOPS!* series. Mike has been helping folks use computers for longer than most can remember, and he really doesn't tweak his own AUTOEXEC.BAT and CONFIG.SYS files.

Introduction

Welcome to the *Absolute Beginner's Guide to Memory Management*! This book is designed to help normal folks like you and me understand how memory is used in our computer systems, and how best to manage that memory to make our PCs run as efficiently as possible.

Why do you need to know about memory management? Well, you don't, really. That is, you don't need to know about memory if you don't care how fast your computer runs, or how much information you can store while your computer is on. However, if you don't manage your memory efficiently, you just don't get the most out of your computer. It's as simple as that.

Fortunately, it really isn't that hard to manage your computer's memory. You need to know a little bit about how memory works, and you need to know how to edit a few of your computer's system files. (I'll show you all you need to know about this stuff, if you don't know it already.) After that, it's a simple matter to follow the instructions in this book, and before you know it, your computer will be running faster and more efficiently (because you'll be an expert memory manager)!

Stuff You'll Find in This Book

This book is divided into three sections. The first section, "Twenty Questions About Memory Management," is the fastest, easiest way to learn about what memory is and how it works. The twenty chapters in this section answer the most common questions about memory asked by absolute beginners.

The second section, "Managing Your System's Memory," shows you how to manage your system's memory. You'll learn how to edit your system files, use various memory managers (including those included with DOS), and add memory to your system.

The third section, "Easy Memory Setups Anyone Can Do," shows you the best memory setups for various system configurations. You'll find a chapter devoted to your particular system, and the recommended way for you to set up your memory.

After all of this, I've included a short glossary of memory-related terms. So if you don't know what the heck I'm talking about, turn to the glossary to learn the basic technobabble. (Although I promise to use as little technobabble as possible, sometimes it can't be avoided when you're talking about basically technical topics!)

Stuff You *Won't* Find in This Book

This book is meant to be a nontechnical guide to memory management. As such, I'll try to avoid as much technical mumbo-jumbo as possible. (I kind of prefer to write in plain English, thank you.) I'll also avoid some real technical topics, on the assumption that you want to know the basic techniques to manage your memory, not esoteric technical tweaks that don't have a big payoff.

There are some other things you won't find in this book. Because this is a book aimed at DOS users, you won't find information on other operating systems, such as OS/2 and UNIX. (Windows is covered extensively, however, because it's an operating *environment* that works alongside DOS.) I don't go into much detail on alternatives to Microsoft's MS-DOS, such as DR DOS and various third-party memory managers. And, because it's a very technical topic, I don't cover memory management in a networked environment. (If you're on a network, ask your network administrator to help with your machine's memory management.)

In short, this is a book that covers the basics—in a basic fashion. If that annoys you, go buy another book.

Who Ought to Be Reading the Stuff in This Book

The title of this book says it all. If you've never tried to manage your memory before (or didn't even know that you could!), you're an absolute beginner at memory management, and this book was written for you.

However, even if you do know a little bit about computer memory, I think you can still get a lot out of this book. In fact, I've aimed this book at three groups of people:

1. Users who know nothing about memory management but want to get the most from their computer systems. If this is you, you should start with Section I and read the entire book.
2. Users who know a little about memory management and want some simple instructions on how to set up their specific systems. If this is you, you should start with Section II for basic instructions, then turn to Section III for specific system setups.
3. Users who know a lot about memory management and want to maximize their memory as quickly and efficiently as possible. If this is you, you can turn right to Section III to find the best memory setup for your specific system.

Conventions Used to Make This Stuff Understandable

Okay, here's the boring section about how to actually decipher all the technical stuff in this book. (Sorry about all this, but the editors made me include this section!)

Anything you see on-screen or type into your computer is in a `computer` typeface.

Special text that may or not bear directly on the regular text is set aside with an icon, as follows:

Yikes!

A *Yikes!* is a caution or warning about a specific operation. Pay attention to these!

This is a tip that might prove useful for what you're about to do.

This is a thought-provoking note. Ignoring these things probably won't hurt you any, but I think they're kind of interesting, anyway!

Skip This, It's Technical!

This is a technical note that more experienced users might find interesting, but you can safely skip over if you want to.

Getting Started on Your Adventure

You really don't need to be a computer expert to maximize your memory usage. Remember, the most famous memory experts are elephants—they're not technical wizards (or even that smart!), but they never, ever forget what's important. So take this book at your own pace (slow and plodding, like our friend the elephant, is okay as far as I'm concerned!), and sooner or later you'll be managing your memory like a computer pro. Turn the page and I'll start answering all your questions about computer memory!

Part I

Twenty Questions About Memory Management

You're an absolute beginner when it comes to memory management. Heck, you're not even sure what memory is! (If you're like me, you have trouble remembering your phone number, let alone details about your computer's memory setup.) So, let's learn a little bit (not a whole lot) about computer memory, by playing a game of Twenty Questions. You ask the questions, I'll provide the answers. Ready to start? Okay, turn the page, and let's go to the first question.

1

What Is Memory?

Boy, you had to start with a tough question, didn't you? Couldn't you think of something a little easier, like, "How's the weather?" or "Is it bigger than a breadbox?" No, you had to delve right into the hard stuff. Well, I guess that's only fair, so give me a minute to compose myself and I'll tell you all about memory—computer memory, that is.

Memory Basics

Memory in your computer isn't all that different than human memory. Computer memory is really nothing more than temporary storage for the data and instructions that your computer uses to do its job.

Skip This, It's Technical!

You'll see the word *storage* used a lot in this book. There are actually two types of storage in your computer system—the temporary storage provided by memory chips, and the more permanent storage provided by your hard and floppy disks. See Chapter 4, "How Does Memory Differ from Disk Space?" for more information about the differences and similarities of disks and memory.

In your computer's memory, instructions and data are stored electronically. That's right, all the important stuff in your computer is nothing more than a series of ephemeral electronic impulses. (Doesn't seem very reassuring, does it?)

In the case of computer memory, all data is converted to what are called *bits* of data. Computers work on the *binary* principle—everything is translated into a 1 or a 0. As far as your computer is concerned, a 1 is an "on" electrical impulse, and a 0 is an "off" impulse (actually, the lack of an impulse).

Now, you wouldn't think a 1 or a 0 can represent a whole lot of data—and you're right! But when you start adding up the bits, you can see how larger amounts of data can be stored. For example, two bits can actually represent four different binary combinations—00, 01, 10, or 11. Three bits gives you even more combinations—000, 001, 010, 011, 100, 101, 110, or 111. When you consider that the typical computer system contains literally millions of bits, you can see how lots and lots of complex information can easily be stored using nothing more than on and off impulses.

PSST!

You can figure out the number of possible combinations for any number of bits by raising 2 to the power of the number of bits; for example, 2 bits is 2 to the second power, or four combinations. Three bits is 2 to the third power, or eight combinations.

Measuring Memory

As you can see, a single bit of memory is relatively unimportant in the grand scheme of things. You need lots and lots of bits just to store small amounts of data or simple instructions.

When you're talking about lots and lots of bits, it's best to use the proper terminology. For example, a group of eight bits is called a *byte* (pronounced bite). A byte allows 256 different binary combinations and is generally large enough to represent a single character like a number or a letter. Expanding on this, you can see that a ten-letter word needs 10 bytes of storage. If you want to store a sentence of 50 characters, you need 50 bytes of memory. A paragraph might require 400 bytes of storage, and a whole page might need 2,000 bytes or more.

It's pretty clear, then, that you need lots of bytes to represent lots of characters. I'm talking thousands of bytes to store anything important.

Table 1.1. Storage units.

Unit	*Size*
byte	8 bits
kilobyte	1,024 bytes
megabyte	1,048,576 bytes
gigabyte	1,073,741,824 bytes

The term for a thousand bytes is a *kilobyte*, which is often abbreviated as K, as in 640K. A thousand kilobytes (approximately a million bytes) is called a *megabyte*. The common abbreviation for megabyte is M or MB, as in 8M. (Computer nerds often call a megabyte a "meg," for short.) If you want to talk about really large amounts of data, you can talk about a thousand megabytes, which is called a *gigabyte*. Now, that's a lot of 1s and 0s!

Skip This, It's Technical!

Actually, a kilobyte is not exactly a thousand bytes, but rather 1,024 bytes because of the "2 to the nth power" business, which gives you 1,024 when you take 2 to the power of 10 (2x2x2x2x2x2x2x2x2x2=1,024). Go figure!

The more memory your computer has, the more data you can store and the more complex the instructions your computer can transmit. In short, with more memory you can do more with your computer.

How Memory Works

So, how do all those bits and bytes manage your computer's memory? It's simple, really. Your computer contains several *memory chips* that do nothing more than store these electronic on and off impulses. When your computer is turned on, various parts of your computer system send impulses to the memory chips, which store them until they are needed by other parts of your computer.

A chip is a miniaturized, silicon-based, transistorized device that plugs into the big *motherboard* in your computer's system unit. There are lots of different kinds of chips, each performing specific functions. Some perform *active* operations (such as the video chip, which controls your system's display) and others perform more *passive* operations (such as memory chips). The most important chip on your motherboard is the *microprocessor* chip, which controls your entire system.

The main microprocessor chip in your computer system is really the brains of the whole operation. It controls all the operations of your system, including what is stored in memory. In fact, the microprocessor ultimately knows where every single byte of memory is located.

The location of each byte is called an *address* (your microprocessor decides on the address for each byte of data). In reality, your system is continually putting new data into memory and removing old data from memory. As long as your computer is turned on, your memory chips are constantly moving around large amounts of data. When you turn your computer off, all the data vanishes. After all, electrical impulses can only be transmitted in the presence of electricity!

Skip This, It's Technical!

There are different types of microprocessor chips that operate at different speeds and handle different amounts of memory. The older chips are called 8088/8086 chips, and they haven't been produced for a number of years. (If you have an older computer, however, it may still use this type of chip.) Newer, faster chips go by the designations 80286, 80386, and 80486. The larger the number of the chip, the faster it runs, and the more memory it can efficiently handle. (You need to know what kind of chip you have in your system in order to maximize your memory usage, as explained in Section III, "Easy Memory Setups Anyone Can Do.")

Wrapping It All Up

Well, the short answer to your first question is that memory is nothing more than a series of electrical impulses used to temporarily store data and instructions used by your computer system. No doubt that raises a lot more questions—19 more, as a matter of fact! So read on to learn even more about your computer's memory.

2

Why Is Memory Important?

Your computer has lots of different ways to store data and instructions. Your system no doubt includes floppy disk drives, which let you plug in an infinite number of floppy disks, each capable of holding more than a megabyte of portable information.

Your system probably also includes a hard disk that can store hundreds of megabytes of data—much more than your computer memory can store. Many newer systems even include an optical disk drive, which reads data from CD-ROM disks, each of which can hold dozens of times more data than a typical hard disk. With all this storage available on your system, why is computer memory so important?

Memory Is Fast

First, all those other types of storage are *electromechanical* in nature. That is, they require some kind of physical interaction to read or write data to the medium. Anytime you require some kind of physical or mechanical movement, things slow down.

In the case of disk storage, the data is magnetically embedded on a hard platter. The disk drive must move an arm out to the spinning platter to physically search for and retrieve the correct data. With chip-based memory, there are no moving parts; the information is stored and retrieved electronically.

Skip This, It's Technical!

The amount of time it takes to locate one bit of stored data is called the *access time*, which is measured in *nanoseconds* (one billionth of a second). The access time for computer memory is normally anywhere from 70 to 120 nanoseconds. Access times for hard disks are thousands of times slower (this is measured in *milliseconds*, or thousandths of seconds—compare this to the billionths of seconds used to measure memory).

In short, the fastest way to get something done on your computer is through the memory, not through a disk drive. When data has to be read off a disk, it takes thousands of times longer than the almost-instantaneous access available if the data is in memory. So the goal of your computer system is to put as much stuff in memory as possible to avoid the wait involved with reading it from disk.

Memory Is Transitory

Memory is great for temporarily storing data and instructions. Disk drives are used if you need more permanent storage. For all those commands and instructions that move from one part of your system to another without needing to be stored forever, memory is the perfect short-term storage medium. Why bother storing something permanently if it only needs to be stored temporarily? Your system sends short-term data to memory instead of to slower long-term disk space. This is a much more efficient use of your system's resources.

Memory Is in the Middle of Things

If you have to have a middleman (or, not to be sexist, a middle-person), it might as well be your system's memory. You see, your computer executes thousands of instructions per second. Your computer's microprocessor can only do one thing at a time, even though it does things very fast, which means that things back up. So, to keep from losing data and instructions, your microprocessor needs some place to store these extra instructions until it can get to them. This is where your computer's memory comes in.

Your microprocessor uses your computer's memory as a kind of middleman that temporarily takes care of all these backed-up instructions. In essence, your memory chips juggle these instructions until your microprocessor can get around to them. If you didn't have excess memory, your computer just wouldn't work—too many instructions would get dropped out of the queue.

Memory Makes Your Programs Go

Because memory is in the middle of things, it only makes sense that your programs make use of its temporary storage capabilities.

To run, most programs load part of themselves (the parts required to get things going) into memory. This way, your computer can have immediate access to the program without having to read it from disk (which, as you may recall, is much slower than reading from memory). The bigger the program, the more memory it tries to use. If you don't have enough system memory, some programs might not even be able to load, let alone run quickly.

Memory Keeps Your Data in Order

When you create a new computer file—for example, a word processing document—the data that you type is kept in your system's memory. In fact, until you save it to disk, the only place the document exists is in memory. If you didn't have any system memory, you wouldn't be able to create any documents!

Graphics require more memory than text. Documents that mix text with lots of graphics require the most memory. The bigger and more complex the document, the more memory you need.

Wrapping It All Up

Add it all up and you can see why memory is important. You need memory because it's a fast way to hold temporary data and instructions—including parts of your programs and all of your files while you're working on them. Without memory, your computer wouldn't be much good at all. The more memory you have, the more efficiently your computer runs. Got all that? Good!

3

Where Is My System's Memory?

Actually, this is kind of a complex question. You see, the data stored in memory exists only as a series of electrical impulses, so it really isn't anywhere. It is somewhere, but that somewhere is in the electrical impulses that are bouncing around inside your memory chips. So your memory is really inside your system's memory chips. Confused? Well, let's try to clear things up.

Pass the Chips!

There are lots of chips inside your computer's system unit. Your system memory is stored on what are called *RAM* chips. RAM stands for *random-access memory*—the name comes from the fact that your microprocessor can access this memory randomly—that is, in any particular order.

Skip This, It's Technical!

There are actually several types of random-access memory. SRAM stands for *static random-access memory;* DRAM stands for *dynamic random-access memory;* and VRAM stands for *video random-access memory*. The most common type of RAM for your system unit is DRAM. VRAM is most often used in high-end video cards. You won't find much SRAM around, except in high-priced computers as super-fast *cache memory* that sits between DRAM chips and your microprocessor.

There are four primary styles of RAM chips used in personal computers (see Figure 3.1):

DIP *Dual in-line package.* This is one of the two most common types of chips. This chip is shaped like a flat rectangle with a lot of metal legs and kind of looks like a spider. DIPs plug into little sockets on your motherboard.

SIMM *Single in-line memory module.* A SIMM is kind of like a miniature expansion card, a few inches long, that has nine RAM chips presoldered to the card. A SIMM doesn't have legs; it has an edge connector and slides into a SIMM socket on your motherboard.

SIP *Single in-line package.* A SIP is a long, multichip chip, kind of like a SIMM. The big difference between a SIMM and a SIP is that a SIP has a single row of legs instead of an edge connector.

ZIP *Zigzag in-line package.* A ZIP is a SIP with two rows of legs staggered on the same edge of the chip.

Find the Chips!

Okay, now you know what RAM chips look like. If you're curious, take the top off your system unit (unplug it first, of course) and look for your chips. So where the heck are they?

The first thing to know is that RAM chips plug into sockets located on the motherboard of your computer. (The motherboard is the big board at the bottom of your system unit that pretty much everything else in your system plugs into.) Most PCs have at least one bank of sockets (in sets of 9, 18, or 36) to hold RAM chips.

Not all of the RAM chip sockets have to be filled for your PC to work. In fact, it's common for your system to have empty sockets to accommodate the addition of extra memory.

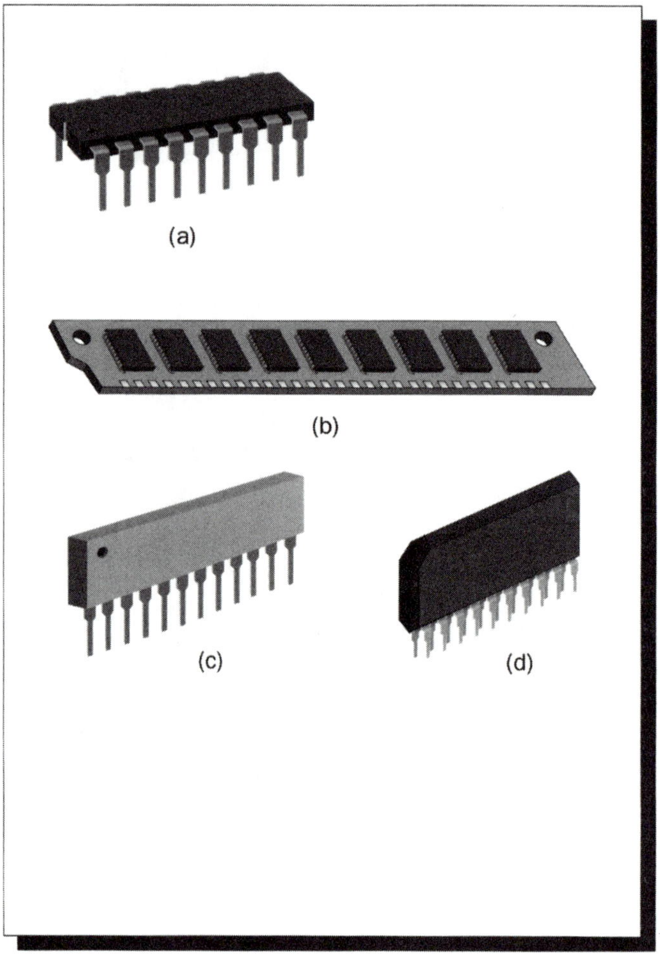

Figure 3.1.
Examples of a DIP (a), a SIMM (b), a SIP (c), and a ZIP (d) chip.

Now, where is that bank of RAM chip sockets? Well, chips are in different places in different computers. (You didn't expect a simple answer, did you?)

For example, Figure 3.2 shows the layout of an IBM PC/AT; the RAM chip banks are in the bottom-left area of the motherboard. Note, however, that there really isn't such a thing as a standard motherboard layout, which means that your chips could be anywhere. The only things you know for sure is that the chip sockets are in banks, and that you can use the guide in Figure 3.1 to identify the chips by their looks.

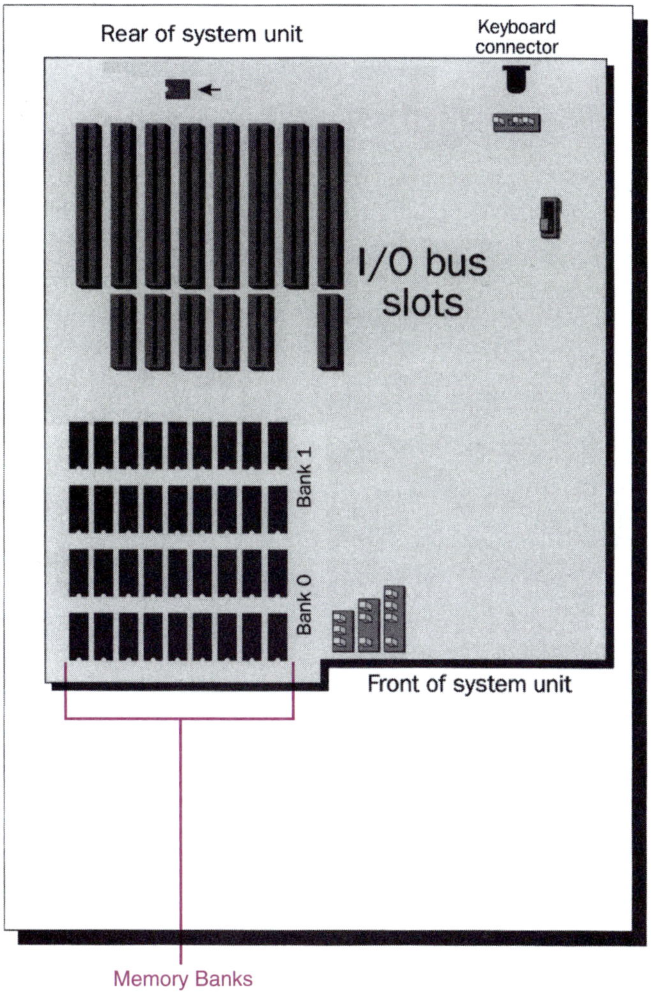

Figure 3.2.
The RAM chip bank of an IBM PC/AT motherboard.

PSST! If you want to find out a lot more about your RAM chips—including how to add more to your system—see Chapter 19, "How Do I Add More Memory?"

Wrapping It All Up

Okay, now you know where your memory is. It's inside all your RAM chips, which are plugged into sockets on your system's motherboard—and your RAM chips are somewhere on your motherboard. Of course, there are lots of other things hooked up to your motherboard, including your system's hard disk driver. Read on to Chapter 4, "How Does Memory Differ from Disk Space?" to learn more about how disks and chips are different (yet vaguely similar).

4

How Does Memory Differ from Disk Space?

This is one of the most common questions asked by absolute beginners (and even by experienced users). After all, don't memory and disks both store data?

Well, yes, they both store data, but in different ways and for different purposes. The differences between memory and disk storage are greater than their similarities.

Disks Can Be Hard

Let's start by looking at exactly what disks are and what they do. First off, there are two basic types of disks: *hard disks* and *floppy disks*. They both work pretty much the same way and do pretty much the same thing. They both serve as long-term storage for large amounts of data. They store data *physically*, as opposed to the electronic storage method used by memory chips.

Hard Disks: Permanent Data Storage

The hard disk is where all of your important data is permanently stored. Hard disks can store up to 200M (much more on some disks) of data. Your hard disk is plugged into your motherboard in your computer's system unit.

The hard disk is made up of numerous metallic platters. These platters store data magnetically. A special read/write *head* realigns magnetic particles on the platters, much like a recording head records data onto magnetic recording tape.

Data is recorded on your hard disk in circular *tracks*, like the tracks on a record album or compact disc. In addition, each disk is divided into *sectors* (see Figure 4.1). The intersections of tracks and sectors are used to locate individual pieces of data on the disk. This tracking data is stored in a special section of your disk called the *file allocation table* (FAT). Your system refers to the FAT data to find specific data on your hard disk.

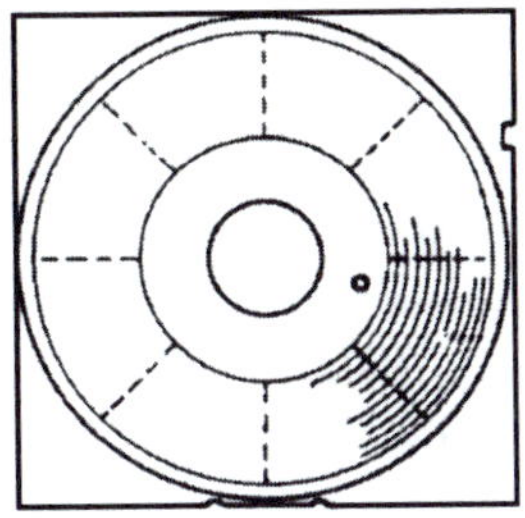

Figure 4.1.
Sectors and tracks on a hard disk.

PSST! Before any disk can be used, it must be *formatted*. When you format a disk, you prepare each track and sector to accept data and create a blank FAT. If a disk has not been formatted, it cannot accept data. Use the DOS `FORMAT` command to format disks.

Floppy Disks: Portable Data Storage

Your computer also includes one or more *floppy disk drives*. These drives accept removable disks of one of four types: 3.5-inch low-density, 3.5-inch high-density, 5.25-inch low-density, and 5.25-inch high-density disks (see Figure 4.2). These floppy disks work much like hard disks, except that they use thin sheets of magnetic tape-like material instead of hard metallic platters. (This is why they're called *floppies*—the material is fairly floppy, compared to a hard disk.)

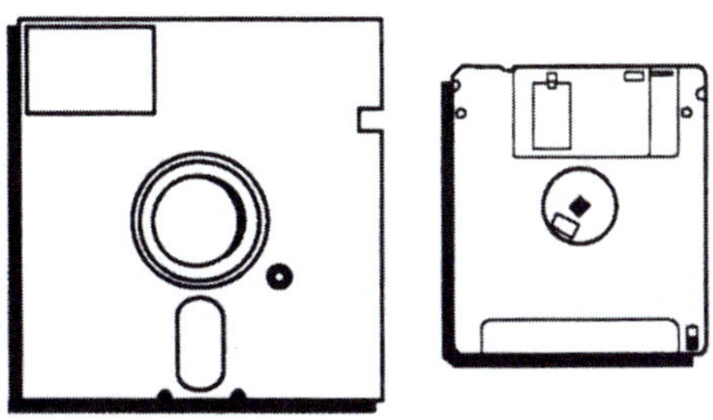

Figure 4.2.
A 5.25-inch disk, left, *and a 3.5-inch disk,* right.

Floppy disks store anywhere from 360K (5.25-inch low-density) to 1.44M (3.5-inch high-density) of data. Because floppy disks are more portable than hard disks, they are often used to store data that must be transported from PC to PC. They are also used to store backup copies of data from your PC's hard disk. For safety's sake, these backup disks should be stored away from your computer, in case of physical damage to your PC.

The heads in the disk drives work just like the read/write head in a hard disk drive. The only difference is that the disk drives are not sealed from the elements like a hard disk drive. This means that disk drives are even more susceptible to dirt, dust, and smoke. If you notice a lot of read/write errors when using floppy disks, the disk drive might need to be realigned or replaced.

Disks Versus Memory: The Head-to-Head Face-Off

Okay, now you know what disks are and what they do. You also know (from the previous three chapters of this wonderful book) what memory is and how it works. But, if you're like me, you're still a little confused about the two—what are the real differences and similarities?

The first big difference is that system memory stores data temporarily—disks store data on a more permanent basis. You see, memory vanishes when you computer is turned off; data stored on a disk stays there through thick and thin, power or no power, until you physically erase the data.

Memory is great for storing data that changes frequently, such as instructions read from your hard disk and not yet fed into your microprocessor, or bits and chunks of your software programs. It isn't great for data you need to keep for awhile—that's why disks exist.

Another difference between the two storage media is that disks (hard disks, especially) can store much more data than your system's memory. Even the most loaded computers today have only between 8M to 16M of memory storage. The average hard disk has 200M storage or more. This makes sense, of course, when you consider that your hard disk has to store things permanently; it just needs more storage space than your memory.

The storage methods used by memory and disks are different. Disks store data physically using magnetic recording methods on either metal or magnetic tape platters. Memory stores data electronically on computer chips.

This last difference accounts for huge differences in the speeds of the different storage media. Simply put, memory is faster than storage. Measured in terms of access time, memory is thousands of times faster than hard disks—the difference between nanoseconds and milliseconds. So if your computer wants something fast, it uses memory. If it wants something stored for a long time, it uses a disk.

Skip This, It's Technical!

A nanosecond is one billionth of a second. A millisecond is one millionth of a second. Therefore, a nanosecond is one thousand times shorter than a millisecond.

Let's tie a ribbon around this with Table 4.1, which lists the features and capabilities of memory and disk storage. This should help you focus on the important differences and similarities between the two forms of data storage.

Table 4.1. Differences between memory and disks.

Characteristic	*Memory*	*Disks*
Usage	Temporary storage	Permanent storage
Speed	Fast	Slow
Amount of storage space	Small	Large
Storage method	Electronic	Physical

Wrapping It All Up

Well, I hope that clears things up for you. In short, memory is used to store data that is temporary in nature and needs to be retrieved quickly (and frequently). Disks are used to store more permanent data, and, therefore, they work more slowly than memory chips.

In reality, you don't have to worry about the differences because your computer (and your operating system) figures out which type of storage is best in a given situation and chooses accordingly.

5

How Does My Computer Use Memory?

If you've read the previous four chapters, you already know that your computer uses memory to store data on a temporary basis. On a very basic level, your microprocessor works in conjunction with your operating system to put data into memory and get it out when it's needed. Of course, the process isn't really as simple as that, so I'll take a few pages and delve into exactly how your computer does all this.

Putting It In

Your microprocessor (also called the *central processing unit*, or *CPU*) is the brains in your computer system. When you first turn on your computer, the CPU takes control and turns on all the other parts of your system, makes sure they're working properly, and sits back and waits for something to do.

That something to do is dictated by your *operating system*, which is loaded into memory when your system is turned on. Your operating system is kind of like a traffic cop by directing instructions from here to there and acting as a middleman between you (or your software programs) and your microprocessor. For most users, the operating system is called *MS-DOS* (or just *DOS* for short). DOS works with your CPU to make your system work. An important part of what your system does is manage memory.

Getting the Right Address on the Right Block

Before I get into how DOS and your CPU load data into memory, you need to know that memory in your computer is divided into small chunks. Each chunk of memory is called a *block*—you can think of a block as a little bucket in your computer just waiting to be filled with data.

I like to think of memory blocks as arranged in rows and columns (see Figure 5.1). This way each bucket has a unique designation determined by the intersection of a particular row and column. This designation is called an *address*, which is used by DOS and the CPU to store and find specific data in memory.

Figure 5.1.
Each memory block has a unique address.

Skip This, It's Technical!

Memory addresses are assigned in hexadecimal notation. Remember *binary* notation, where everything is either a 0 or a 1? Well, hexadecimal notation represents a *base sixteen* numbering system. Instead of using just two characters (as in the binary system) or ten characters (as in the normal decimal system), this numbering system uses sixteen characters! The characters used are the numerals 0 through 9 and the letters A through F. This results in addresses that look like "0CD65" and "F8000."

Taking the Bus

Now you know that memory is chunked into blocks and identified by addresses. But how does the memory get from your CPU to your memory chips?

The route between parts of your system is called a *bus*. (I'm not sure why; a bus is really nothing more than a group of wires.) The best way to visualize a bus is as a freeway on which data travels. Bus size is measured in bits—the bigger the bus (that is, the wider the freeway), the more data (cars) that can be moved at any one time. Although there are lots of different kinds of buses, I'll only talk about the one that matters for memory management.

The route between your microprocessor and all other system components is called the *external data bus*. Different types of microprocessors have data buses of different sizes. In today's computers, the external data bus ranges from 8 bits (in old 8088-based systems) to 32 bits (in 80386 and 80486 systems). Obviously, the bigger the data bus, the faster the system operates—one reason why the newer 32-bit systems run so much faster than older 8- or 16-bit PCs.

HMM... Every CPU also has an *internal data bus*, which moves data between the internal components of your microprocessor.

The external data bus (like all buses) also carries the addresses to which data is being written or read. Not surprisingly, different buses can carry different numbers of addresses. The more addresses carried, the more memory that can be accessed. Older 8088-based PCs can only address 1M of memory; the slightly newer 80286-based PCs can address 16M of memory; and the newest 80386- and 80486-based PCs can address a whopping 4,096M of memory (see Table 5.1)! So the newer your PC, the more memory you can use in your system.

Table 5.1. **CPUs and their buses.**

CPU	*External Data Bus*	*Memory Addressability*
8088	8-bit	1M
8086	16-bit	1M
80286	16-bit	16M
80386SX	16-bit	16M
80386	32-bit	4,096M
80486	32-bit	4,096M

The bottom line: the newer your PC, the faster it runs and the more memory it can address. Got that? Good.

How It All Fits Together

From here it's actually pretty simple. DOS looks at everything that's happening on your system and decides what should go into memory—program instructions, documents, whatever. DOS then instructs your CPU to place certain data at a certain memory address. Your CPU complies, sending the data through the external data bus to your memory chip. The data is then placed in the specified address (where it stays until it is needed). And that's that.

Getting It Out

Getting data out of memory is the reverse of putting it in. DOS decides it needs the data and instructs the CPU to retrieve it from the specified address. The data is then transferred through the external data bus back to the CPU, where it is ultimately routed someplace else (to the screen, printer, or hard disk, for example).

Freeing It Up

When you exit a program or close a document, these instructions and data are no longer needed in memory. Your microprocessor then frees the memory blocks that hold this data, essentially emptying the buckets so new data can be stored.

Yikes!

Some poorly behaved programs may not allow all their memory blocks to be freed when you close the program. This means that you have less memory available than you might think, given what programs are running at the time. The worst offenders appear to be Windows programs, such as Ami Pro and Word for Windows. You may need to reboot your computer from time to time to free up these inaccessible memory blocks.

Wrapping It All Up

You start your computing session with a bunch of empty memory blocks. As things happen (dictated by either you or your computer programs), DOS works with your CPU to move data into and out of specific memory blocks.

It sounds simple, but it requires an awful lot of computing power. The thing that amazes me is that all this is happening in the background, automatically, without you or me ever knowing that it's going on. Memory management truly is an amazing thing, isn't it?

6

What Does DOS Have to Do with Memory?

To effectively manage your memory, you need to know a little bit about your system's operating system. As you'll see, DOS has a lot to do with memory.

A Little Background on DOS

You can have lots and lots of software programs on your system, but there is one essential program you must have for your system to operate. This program is the *operating system*; the most popular operating system used today is called *MS-DOS* (or just *DOS* for short).

What an Operating System Does

DOS, like any operating system, acts as the interface between you (and your software programs) and your system's microprocessor. DOS figures out what needs to be done and tells the CPU what to do. Your CPU then does all the work—including reading and writing data to and from memory.

Unlike other software programs, DOS starts automatically when you turn on your computer system. When your system starts, it accesses DOS and reads two *system files* (also called configuration files) that give DOS some basic instructions on how to configure and run your system (including how to configure your system's memory). These two files are called AUTOEXEC.BAT and CONFIG.SYS, and you'll be reading a lot about them throughout this book, especially in Section II, "Managing Your System's Memory."

The Four Faces of DOS

DOS is actually not a single piece of software, but rather four separate components that work together to operate your system:

- **The basic input/output system (BIOS).** BIOS is the core of DOS that interacts directly with your CPU.
- **The command interpreter.** This is the "command line" that lets you input specific commands, which are then interpreted by the BIOS into language your hardware can understand.
- **The DOS utilities.** These utilities are special miniprograms that let you perform specific tasks, such as formatting disks.
- **The DOS Shell.** This is the friendly face of DOS (available with DOS 4.0 and later versions): a menu-driven interface that tries to make DOS a little simpler to use.

Different Versions of DOS

Throughout the past twelve years there have been various versions of DOS, as Microsoft (the company that developed DOS and got rich off of it) upgraded its performance and usability. The first version of DOS was labeled 1.0; the most recent version is 6.0.

The earliest versions of DOS really didn't have much in the way of memory management capabilities; it wasn't until DOS 5.0 that you could use DOS to efficiently manage your memory use. With the latest upgrade, DOS 6.0, Microsoft has included some features that make managing memory even easier than before.

PSST!

Suffice to say, if you're running an older version of DOS, you probably should upgrade to DOS 6.0 ASAP!

How DOS Works with Memory

Because DOS controls what happens on your system, it only stands to reason that it has a good deal of control over your system's memory usage. Let's look at how DOS impacts your memory management.

Getting Loaded with DOS

First and foremost, you need to know that DOS itself uses memory! That's right, DOS is like most other programs in that it loads vital instructions into your system's memory when it starts. These instructions are loaded into the lowermost part of your system's memory.

Skip This, It's Technical!

The main parts of DOS that are loaded into system memory are the COMMAND.COM programs and two "hidden" programs associated with the DOS BIOS routines. This is why you need COMMAND.COM and the two BIOS files on any disk you're using to boot your computer. Without these files, they can't be loaded into memory, and DOS can't run.

After it loads itself into memory, DOS then partitions off an area of memory for it to use to keep track of open files. (This area is called the *system data area.*) Next, DOS loads various *device drivers* into memory, and returns control of your system over to you, via the infamous DOS prompt: C>.

Device drivers are special programs that control various peripherals in your computer system, such as your video display, printer, and mouse.

The DOS Memory Limit

When DOS was first developed, microprocessors couldn't handle any more than 1M of memory. (Take a look back at Chapter 5, "How Does My Computer Use Memory?" to figure out why; remember that the earliest PCs used either 8088 or 8086 microprocessors.) They also didn't think that any software program would ever use more than 640K of memory. All the programs back then were relatively small.

DOS' developers configured the operating system to efficiently use 1M of RAM, with only 640K of that devoted to program use. This 640K program barrier is often called the *DOS memory limit* because it divides what is called *conventional memory* (less than 640K) with what is called *upper system memory* (between 640K and 1M).

The way it works is that all your program data is loaded into the first 640K of system memory. The area above 640K is reserved for DOS' use. Note, however, that DOS itself, as well as all device drivers and the system data area, is actually in conventional memory, which means that you really don't have a full 640K available for your programs. (Depending on your system, you probably have anywhere from 420K to 620K of conventional memory free.) After DOS is loaded, your memory looks something like Figure 6.1.

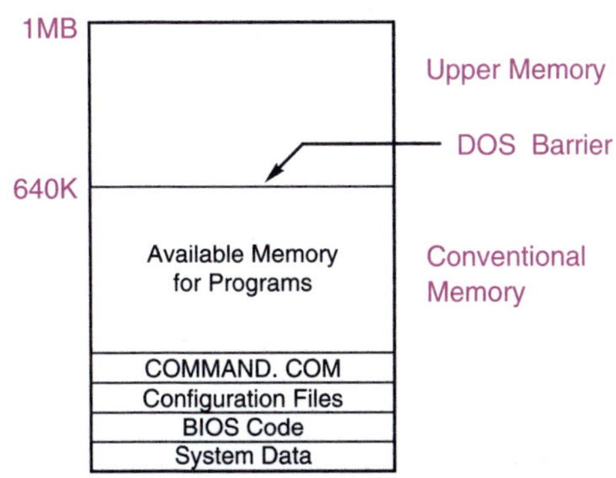

Figure 6.1.
Conventional and upper memory.

How DOS Affects Memory Usage

Remember when I said that DOS reserves the area above 640K for its own use? Well, it uses some of this area for things like BIOS code and video management. But when all is said and done, DOS just can't fill all the upper memory, which leaves some spare memory that can be used for other purposes.

With the newer versions of DOS (Version 5.0 and later) you can instruct DOS to use these spare *upper memory blocks* to store temporary data from your programs or device drivers and other small programs.

PSST!

You can also use third-party memory managers to break the DOS 640K memory limit and manage your upper memory. See Chapter 24, "Using Third-Party Memory Managers," for more information.

There is also an area of memory above 1M (called *extended memory*) that newer versions of DOS can access (if you have at least an 80286-based computer). Turn to the next chapter for a more detailed discussion of all the different types of memory.

Where You Do It—The DOS System Files

Remember earlier in this chapter when I mentioned the two DOS system files, AUTOEXEC.BAT and CONFIG.SYS? Well, these really are important files when it comes to memory management. You see, with DOS 5.0 and later versions you can insert commands into these files that impact the memory you use. For example, you can instruct DOS to load various device drivers into upper memory blocks, or even to load DOS itself into extended memory—all with little one-line commands in these system files. See Chapter 22, "Setting Up Your System for Maximum Memory Use," and

Chapter 23, "Working with DOS 6.0 Memory Management Tools," for more detailed instructions on managing your memory with these DOS system files.

Wrapping It All Up

Okay, so here it is. DOS has a lot to do with memory because it both controls memory use and uses memory itself. DOS has a built-in 640K memory limit for program use, but this barrier can be broken with newer versions of DOS (and with third-party mem-ory managers). So, you need to know a little about DOS to effectively manage your memory, which you'll be doing through-out the rest of this book.

7

What Different Kinds of Memory Are There?

Well, folks, there are a lot of different kinds of memory. So, let's just scoot through the list of what's what in the memory world.

Read-Only Memory

Read-only memory (also known as *ROM*) is memory that can be read but not written to. That is, it's electronic memory that is permanently stored on a computer chip.

I won't bother you much with ROM in this book, but there are some uses you might find interesting. For example, your computer has a ROM chip that contains a startup program and your system's basic input/output system (BIOS). This chip actually starts your PC when you flip the On switch; if this chip is damaged, your system won't start!

Random Access Memory

Random access memory (also known as *RAM*) is memory that can be both read from and written to. RAM is the type of memory I'm talking about throughout this book—memory that temporarily stores important data and instructions in your computer system.

RAM is volatile. Whatever is stored in it only exists as long as it has power. When your system is turned off, data stored in RAM disappears.

Skip This, It's Technical!

There are actually three basic types of RAM chips: *dynamic* RAMs (DRAMs), *static* RAMs (SRAMs), and *video* RAMs (VRAMs). DRAMs are the most commonly used chips because they store a large amount of data while consuming very little power. SRAMs are faster than DRAMs, but they cost more to produce and use more power. Some high-end PCs use SRAMs as *cache memory* that sits between normal memory and your CPU to speed up program execution. VRAMs are most often used in high-end video cards to speed the performance of your video display.

Your computer allocates RAM in several different areas (see Figure 7.1).

Figure 7.1.

All the types of memory in your system: conventional, upper, extended, and expanded.

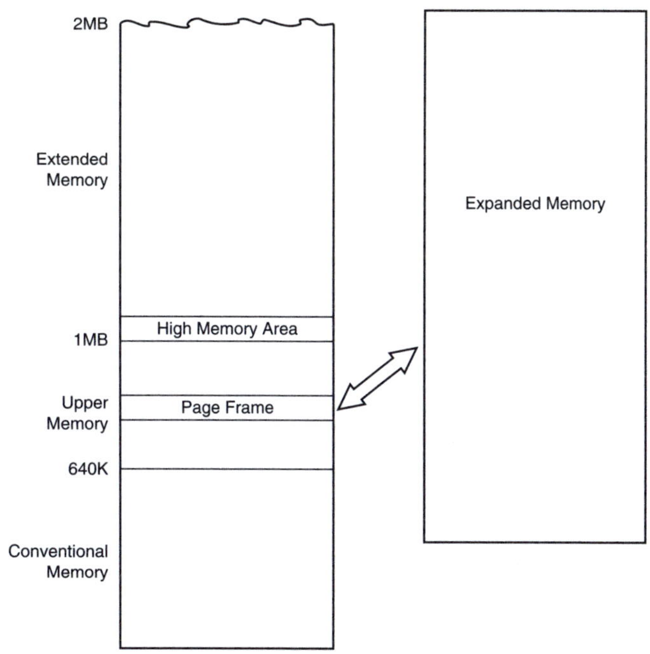

Conventional Memory

Conventional memory is the first 640K of RAM on your system. DOS uses conventional memory to load all your software programs, as well as some basic DOS files.

Upper Memory

Upper memory is the area of RAM between 640K and 1M. DOS uses upper memory to store various BIOS routines, as well as video memory. Because DOS doesn't use all of the upper memory area, there are numerous *upper memory blocks* that can be used (in DOS 5 or later versions) to load device drivers and other small programs.

High Memory

The *high memory area* is the first 64K RAM of extended memory.

Extended Memory

Extended memory is any RAM above the 1M mark.

Expanded Memory

Expanded memory is RAM linked through a special page frame in upper memory to available memory above 1M. Expanded memory was originally used to take advantage of memory above 1M before DOS could access this memory (with the advent of extended memory, expanded memory is infrequently used).

Wrapping It All Up

Well, this chapter should have answered your question about the kinds of memory. You can now turn to the next few chapters, which answer specific questions about specific types of memory.

8

What Is the Difference Between RAM and ROM?

Well, if you read the last chapter you learned the basic definitions of RAM and ROM. But let's take a closer look at each one, and the differences between the two.

What RAM Does

Random access memory (also known as *RAM*) is memory that can be both read from and written to. RAM is memory that temporarily stores important data and instructions in your computer system. RAM only exists as long as it has power—when you turn your system off, any data stored in RAM disappears.

RAM is ideally suited to store information that changes, and RAM is used as your system's main memory, temporarily storing program data and instructions. Computers today have a minimum of 640K RAM and up to 8M RAM or more on some newer models.

There are different types of RAM: *dynamic* RAM (DRAM), which combines low power consumption and affordable price; and *static* RAM (SRAM), which is faster than DRAM but more expensive and more power hungry. DRAM is used for your main system memory; SRAM (when it's used at all) is used as a memory cache between your normal system memory and your CPU to speed up some common operations.

What ROM Does

Read-only memory (also known as *ROM*) is memory that can only be read from, not written to. That is, it's electronic memory that is permanently stored on a computer chip. It isn't volatile like RAM. When you turn off the power, the data stored on a ROM chip continues to exist. ROM is slightly faster than RAM, with access times of approximately 15 nanoseconds (compared to 70-120 nanosecond RAM access times).

Skip This, It's Technical!

Actually, there are certain types of ROM chips that you can write to. These are known generically as *programmable ROMs* (PROMs) and include chips that can also be erased, such as the *erasable programmable ROM* (EPROM) and the *electrically erasable programmable ROM* (EEPROM). None of these PROM chips, however, are used in today's PCs.

ROM is less ideal than RAM for storing data and instructions for your computer system. ROM is ideal, however, for storing information that does not change. For that reason, your PC contains a special ROM chip that holds your system's key startup programs. These prepare your PC for use and load your system's core BIOS (basic input/output system). Having them in ROM means that they're always there—if they were in RAM, they would disappear as soon as you computer was turned off (which means you could never turn it back on again).

Other Types of ROM

There are other types of ROM besides the startup chip. In fact, anytime you don't need to enter or edit data, ROM is an okay means of storage.

DOS on ROM

ROM chips can have a lot of different uses inside your PC. Although the most common ROM chip is the startup chip, there are other uses for the nonvolatile memory provided by ROMs.

For example, some portable PCs include DOS itself on a ROM chip. The advantage of putting DOS on a ROM chip is that it loads very fast and frees up valuable RAM and disk space for program information. The disadvantage is that you can't upgrade your DOS without changing the chip. If you use a portable PC, you know that both RAM and disk space are limited, so putting DOS on a ROM is a pretty good deal.

ROM Cards

Some really small portable PCs don't even have hard disks—there's just not enough room in their notebook-sized cases. In these subnotebook computers, program storage is done via ROM cards. A ROM card is a removable device that looks like a flat circuit board or a cartridge from a video game. This card contains enough ROM to store a complete software program. When you want to run a program, instead of accessing your hard disk (which you don't have on these small PCs), you plug in the software ROM card instead. It's a great way to save resources on portable PCs and still carry all your programs around with you!

CD-ROMs

There is another type of ROM you may have read about that really doesn't have anything to do with memory, although it will be very important to your computer system over the next few years. CD-ROM has nothing to do with memory, but it has a heck of a lot to do with storage of large amounts of data. A CD-ROM disk is like a CD (compact disc) you play on an audio system. Data is encoded via pits on tracks on a shiny metallic disk. A laser beam reads the pits and decodes them into data. (In the case of an audio CD, the data becomes sound.) Data on a CD-ROM can include just about any type of digital data you can imagine—audio, video, computer files, you name it. When a CD-ROM is used as storage for computer files, it functions sort of like a big floppy disk, except that it can contain more than 600M of data!

Skip This, It's Technical!

As if you weren't confused enough, there are actually several different types of CD-ROMs. For example, there are new CD-ROMs from Kodak called Photo CDs, which are used to store photographic images. Although all Photo CD players are compatible with normal computer CD-ROMs, not all CD-ROM players are compatible with Photo CDs. See, I told you this was confusing!

The big difference between a CD-ROM and a disk is that you can't write data to a CD-ROM—it's a read-only medium, just like ROM memory. So, you can only read data from a CD-ROM, which is still okay for a lot of tasks (like playing back large multimedia applications).

Why isn't CD-ROM called CD-ROD (read-only disk)? Beats me. This is just one of those computer terms that really doesn't make a lot of sense, but everybody uses it anyway. Oh well . . . .

The Big Differences Between RAM and ROM

Okay, let's boil down the RAM/ROM differences (see Table 8.1).

Table 8.1. RAM compared with ROM.

Characteristic	*RAM*	*ROM*
Read capability	Yes	Yes
Write capability	Yes	No
Volatile	Yes	No
Speed	Slower	Faster
Storage type	Temporary	Permanent
Ideal for storing	Data that changes frequently	Data that doesn't change

Wrapping It All Up

There you have it. RAM is used for system memory because it's great for data that changes frequently. ROM is only used for data that doesn't change—such as storing your system's startup programs. You want as much RAM as possible on your system. The amount of ROM you have is set when you buy your system.

Remember, though, that both RAM and ROM memory store data electronically, and they are much faster than disk storage.

9

What Is the Difference Between High and Upper Memory?

Boy, there are lots of different kinds of memory, aren't there? I started with RAM and ROM, and now I'm talking about high and upper memory! Well, both high and upper memory are types of RAM, and both are managed by DOS. So read on to find out the real differences between these two memory types.

Upper Memory

As you may recall, DOS originally was designed to handle 1M of RAM. The first 640K is allocated for program data and instructions. The area between 640K and 1M is called *upper memory*, which is reserved for DOS' use.

DOS typically uses upper memory to load various items: the BIOS, hard disk controllers, video BIOS, and video memory. All this together typically adds up to less than 300K of the total 384K space (the balance generally goes unused).

Unfortunately, DOS loads programs and drivers in a noncontiguous fashion, as shown in Figure 9.1. This leaves gaps in the middle of upper memory, as opposed to a single unused area. These gaps are called *upper memory blocks* (UMBs), as shown in Figure 9.1.

Figure 9.1.

Some uses of upper memory blocks.

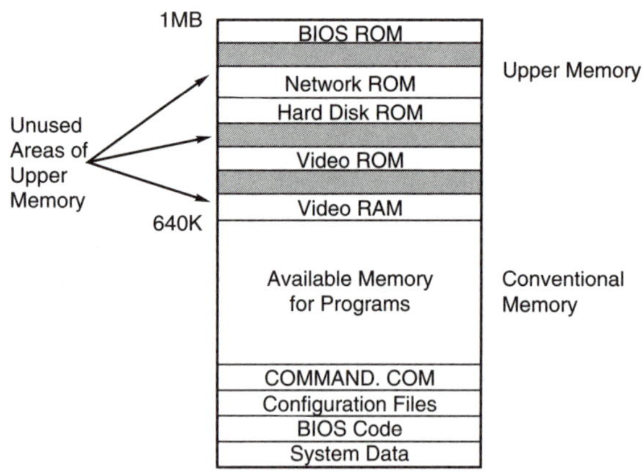

With DOS 5 and 6, however, you can access these upper memory blocks. (You can also use a third-party memory management program to access UMBs). These little chunks of memory are ideal for storing small programs and device drivers. You use special commands in your CONFIG.SYS and AUTOEXEC.BAT files to load these programs into UMBs (see Chapter 21, "Preparing for the Big Setup").

PSST!

UMBs are also good for storing *terminate-and-stay resident* (TSR) programs. These are programs that you load into memory when you start your system so you can quickly recall them at a later time.

High Memory

Beyond the first 1M of RAM is memory that is referred to as *extended memory*. DOS, prior to Version 5.0, could not access this memory. DOS 5.0 and 6.0, however (along with some third-party memory management programs), can access memory beyond 1M.

The first 64K of this extended memory is called the *high memory area* (HMA). If you have a 80286 or better PC, you can easily access this high memory. You need to use a special DOS device driver called HIMEM.SYS, which is included with DOS 5.0 and 6.0 (as well as Microsoft Windows). This driver is loaded via your CONFIG.SYS file (see Chapter 21). The HMA is commonly used to load DOS, although other small programs and device drivers can also fit into this space.

Which Should You Use?

The answer is easy—use both if you can! If you have DOS 5.0 or above (and you really should, shouldn't you?) and an 80286 or better PC, you can use both UMBs and the HMA to load DOS, other small programs, and device drivers high. If you don't use these memory areas, you're just wasting space. If you do use UMBs and the HMA, you're freeing up valuable conventional memory that can now be used to run your programs faster and more efficiently. So if you can, use 'em. Enough said.

Wrapping It All Up

Don't get confused. When it comes to RAM, upper comes before high, which is part of extended. (Got all that?)

High isn't as high as you can go, however. In actuality, high memory is just the first part of extended memory. You can add just as much extended memory to your system as can fit on your motherboard (or that you can afford!). Normally this means 8M to 16M, although some high-end systems have a lot more RAM than that. Read ahead to the next chapter for a discussion of extended (and expanded) memory.

10

What Is the Difference Between Extended and Expanded Memory?

In the last chapter you learned about upper and high memory areas. Now it's time to go beyond high into extended and expanded memory!

The one thing both extended and expanded memory have in common is that they use any memory above the 1M level. That is, they both start right above upper memory. After that, however, the differences begin.

Extended Memory

Extended memory (also called XMS) is RAM beyond the 1M level on any 80286, 80386, or 80486 PC. Unfortunately, DOS wasn't designed to use memory beyond the first 1M, which means that DOS can't directly use this extended memory. Figure 10.1 shows where you can find extended memory—beyond the first 1M.

However, if you have a special *extended memory manager* program, you can access this extended memory. Extended memory managers shift your CPU from *real mode* (which can't use extended memory) to *protected mode* (which can use extended memory). These managers essentially bypass DOS, which can't handle memory addresses above the first 1M, and deal with the extended memory directly, which allows programs to load above the 1M level.

These memory manager programs (which adhere to an industry standard called the *Extended Memory Specification*—abbreviated XMS) can also use extended memory as simple memory storage or trick your system into using extended memory as expanded memory.

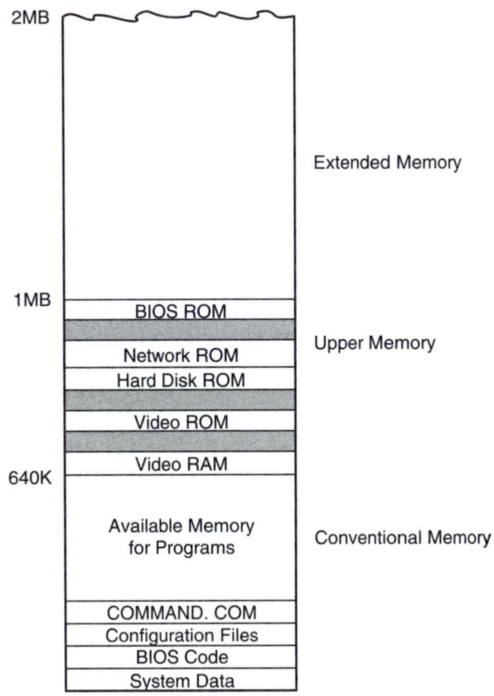

Figure 10.1. *Extended memory—the memory above 1M.*

Skip This, It's Technical!

80286 and higher computers have two modes of operation that affect memory use: *real mode* and *protected mode*. In real mode, the CPU mimics an 8088 chip, using only 1M of RAM, which means extended memory can't be used. In protected mode, the CPU can use as much memory as you have (up to 16M on an 80286; up to 4,096M on an 80386 or 80486).

Numerous DOS software programs incorporate their own extended memory managers. These programs include 1-2-3 Release 3.X and AutoCAD. In addition, the Microsoft Windows operating environment uses as much extended memory as you can give it. (If you don't have enough extended memory, Windows won't run at all!)

Expanded Memory

Expanded memory (also called EMS) is extra memory (above 1M) that, unlike extended memory, can be accessed by DOS. It can't be used for running programs, but it can temporarily store program data.

Expanded memory is accessed via a gateway located in your system's upper memory (see Figure 10.2). This special gateway is called a *page frame*, and it is a 640K area created by an *expanded memory manager*. (This is a device driver loaded via your CONFIG.SYS file, as explained in Chapter 22, "Setting Up Your System for Maximum Memory Use"). Data is continually copied from your expanded memory into the page frame then back again, as shown in Figure 10.2.

In essence, DOS only deals with the memory while it's in the upper memory page frame. DOS can deal with upper memory, but not with memory above 1M. An expanded memory manager essentially tricks DOS into thinking that all it's dealing with is a little area of upper memory, when in fact it's working with as much expanded memory as you have on your system.

Expanded memory managers adhere to an industry standard called the LIM EMS standard. LIM stands for Lotus, Intel, and Microsoft, which jointly developed the standard. Just like software programs, this standard has been updated through the years; the latest version is called EMS 4.0.

Figure 10.2.
Expanded memory is accessed via a page frame.

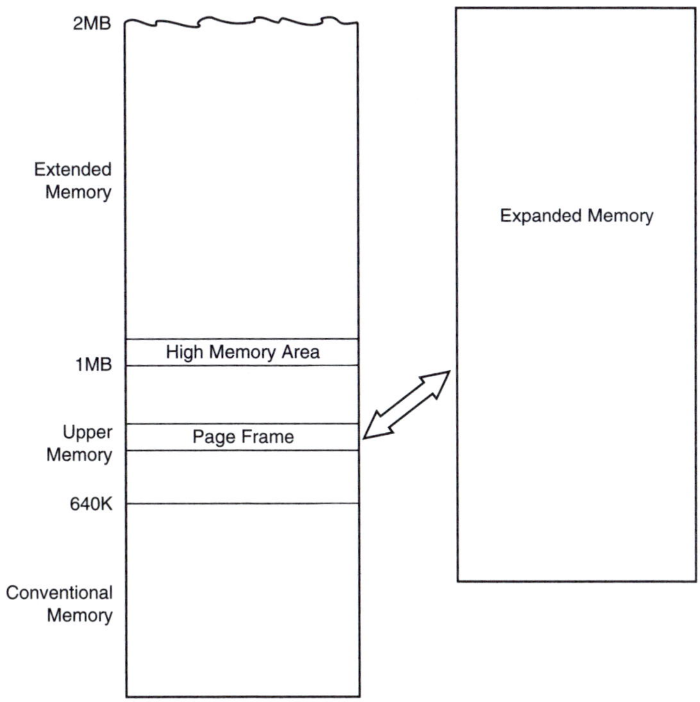

One key thing about expanded memory is that it must be separate from the other memory on your system. That is, you can't just add a few memory chips to your motherboard to get above 1M and use expanded memory. You need to add a special expanded memory expansion card (which plugs into one of your system unit's empty card slots) to add expanded memory to your system. With an expanded memory card and an expanded memory driver, you can use as much as 32M of expanded memory on your system.

Which Should You Use?

Well, whether you use XMS (extended memory) or EMS (expanded memory) really depends on the applications you're using. If your programs are XMS-compatible, you should use XMS. If your programs are EMS-compatible, you should use EMS. It's as simple as that.

Since EMS was developed before XMS, there are more programs available that use EMS than XMS. However, many of these are older programs. More newer programs are being developed that use XMS.

If you're a Windows user, the choice is easy. Windows uses extended memory—period. So if you're using Windows and Windows applications, go for XMS—period.

Wrapping It All Up

The good thing about both extended and expanded memory is that they allow you to access more than just the standard 1M RAM. The more RAM you can access, the faster and more efficiently your computer runs. So if you only have 1M RAM on your computer, trot down to your local computer store and buy some more chips (or an EMS card), then install the proper memory manager and find out just how fast your computer will go!

11

What Is a RAM Disk?

A RAM disk is kind of like a disk drive that resides in memory. With a RAM disk you have the benefit of fast RAM access, even though your computer thinks it's dealing with a physical disk drive. The downside of using a RAM disk is that, like all other RAM, it vanishes when your computer is turned off (or loses power for whatever reason).

How RAM Disks Work

A RAM disk is, technically, a *virtual* disk drive, which means that it just pretends to be a disk drive—the drive only exists in your system's memory.

Your system thinks that the memory area assigned to the RAM disk is actually a real disk drive. If your hard disk is drive C:, for example, your system thinks the RAM disk is another disk drive called D:. It lets you read and write to the RAM disk just like you would a normal hard disk. The difference is that your RAM disk is much faster than your normal hard disk.

Of course, another difference is that your RAM disk is really just a figment of your memory. That is, it's as volatile as anything else in RAM. The disk only exists while the power is on; if you turn your system off, any data on the RAM disk disappears along with any other data stored in RAM.

Yikes!

If you experience a sudden power outage, you'll lose all the data currently stored on the RAM disk. That's one of the great downsides of using a RAM disk.

Creating a RAM Disk

You create a RAM disk by installing a RAM disk driver and loading that driver into memory. You can load the driver in conventional, extended, or expanded memory. (In fact, RAM disks are great ways to use the extended or expanded memory that some regular programs can't touch!) Depending on the version of DOS you're using, the name of the RAM disk driver file is either RAMDRIVE.SYS or VDISK.SYS.

PSST! 

There are other third-party RAM disk utilities available. Some users claim these third-party RAM disks work faster or more reliably than the DOS versions. For me, RAMDRIVE.SYS and VDISK.SYS work just fine.

If you're using DOS 5.0 or 6.0, you use the RAMDRIVE.SYS driver. To load this driver, add some variation of the following command line to your CONFIG.SYS file:

```
DEVICE[HIGH]=C:\DOS\RAMDRIVE.SYS [disksize] [sectorsize]
[direntries] [/E] [/A]
```

This looks a little confusing, but it's really quite simple. You simply use the `DEVICE` or `DEVICEHIGH` command (explained in Chapter 22, "Setting Up Your System for Maximum Memory Use") to load the RAMDRIVE.SYS file from whichever directory it's located in (normally C:\DOS). You can then specify any of the following parameters:

`DISKSIZE`	The size of the RAM disk in kilobytes. The default is 64K.
`SECTORSIZE`	The size of the sectors used for the RAM disk in bytes. The default is 512 bytes.

`DIRENTRIES`	This puts a limit on the number of files and directories that can exist in the root directory of the RAM disk. The default is 64.
`/E`	This switch places the RAM disk in extended memory.
`/A`	This switch places the RAM disk in expanded memory. (If you don't use either switch, the RAM disk is placed in conventional memory.)

So, how does this work in practice? Let's say you want to create a 2M RAM disk in extended memory, with all other parameters at the default values. Add the following line to your CONFIG.SYS file:

```
DEVICE=C:\DOS\RAMDRIVE.SYS 2048 /E
```

If you're using a version of DOS prior to DOS 5.0, use the VDISK.SYS driver. (Of course, my strong advice is if you're using an older version of DOS, upgrade to DOS 6.0 immediately!)

The syntax for loading VDISK.SYS is identical to that of RAMDRIVE.SYS. If you want to create a 2M RAM disk in extended memory, add the following line to your CONFIG.SYS file:

```
DEVICE=C:\DOS\VDISK.SYS 2048 /E
```

When you create your RAM disk, DOS assigns it the next drive letter after your last hard disk drive. If your hard disk is drive C:, your RAM disk will be drive D:.

Using a RAM Disk

You use a RAM disk just like you would a normal disk drive. You can copy files to and from the RAM disk, make subdirectories on it, and so on. The differences are that the RAM disk is much faster than your normal physical disk drives, and it's volatile.

Running a software program from your RAM disk requires a little bit of effort—and strategy. First, you have to copy the program to your RAM disk—every time you boot your computer. Then, when you're done using the program, you have to copy all program files back to your hard disk, or you lose the data. You may find that it's not worth the trouble to run programs from your RAM disk.

A much better use for RAM disks is for programs that frequently access the hard disk with *temporary files*. You see, these programs are really using your hard disk as overflow memory. So why not trick these programs into using memory as a hard disk, which they were trying to use as memory in the first place?

Yikes!

If you do use your RAM disk to store temporary files, you need to add the following line to your AUTOEXEC.BAT file, where `X` is the letter assigned to your RAM disk: `SET TEMP=X:\`

Should You Use a RAM Disk?

Whether or not you use a RAM disk depends on how you're using your computer. Table 11.1 outlines several possible scenarios and my recommendations for each one:

Table 11.1. Should I use a RAM disk?

Scenario	*Use RAM Disk?*
Running Windows	No
No excess memory	No

continues

Table 11.1. continued

Scenario	*Use RAM Disk?*
Excess memory (using EMS or XMS)	Maybe
Excess memory (can't use EMS or XMS)	Yes

Let's examine the reasoning behind all of this. The first data point is whether you have any excess memory. If you don't, forget the RAM disk.

Next, are you effectively using your excess memory—either via extended or expanded memory managers? If so, you probably don't need a RAM disk. This logic also applies if you're running Windows—Windows uses all the extended memory you have, so there's no need for a RAM disk.

If you're not exploiting all your excess memory, then by all means create a RAM disk. Just remember that because it's only temporary, any data you're storing there goes poof when you turn off your PC.

Wrapping It All Up

Well, now you know all about RAM disks. Myself, I don't use 'em. The reason is partly a mixture of fear of losing data during a power outage combined with extremely efficient extended memory use with Windows 3.1. But if you want to create a RAM disk, all power to you (literally!).

Now, if you think RAM disks are fun, turn the page and read all about disk caches!

12

What Is a Disk Cache?

Before you can understand a disk cache, you probably need to understand a little bit about caches in general. A cache (pronounced cash) is a means of storing information temporarily. (Sounds kind of like what memory does, doesn't it?) Caches are usually used to store information that demands repeated access, and they work faster than standard means of storage.

So if your standard means of storage is a hard disk, what is faster? Why, memory, of course! A *disk cache* temporarily stores information in memory that would otherwise be stored on your hard disk. Because memory is faster than hard disk storage, your CPU gets faster access to the data in the disk cache—and your system operates faster.

Another type of cache is called a *memory cache*. This actually uses fast memory (on SRAM chips) to temporarily store frequently accessed memory faster than standard DRAM-based memory. Again, cache works faster than the standard means of storage.

How a Disk Cache Works

A disk cache acts kind of like a buffer for important data. As DOS reads data from your hard disk, a copy of that information is sent to the disk cache in your system's memory. When DOS needs that data again, it goes straight to the cache, where it can access the information from memory much faster than from the hard disk. This way, your computer actually operates faster than normal because the information it uses the most is always right at hand in memory!

You can create a disk cache with a special DOS device driver—the driver that comes with DOS and Windows (called SMARTDrive) or third-party drivers. All disk cache drivers work pretty much the same way: you load them into memory in either the CONFIG.SYS or AUTOEXEC.BAT system files, then they stay in memory doing their jobs in the background while you go about your normal computing tasks.

Yikes!

Here's an important warning if you're using a disk cache: never use more than one disk cache at one time—you'll lose data if you do! You shouldn't load both SMARTDRV.EXE and SMARTDRV.SYS at the same time. (There is only one exception to this rule. If you're using DOS 6 and have a special kind of hard disk—explained in Chapter 22, "Setting Up Your System for Maximum Memory Use"—you should use what is called *double buffering*, which uses both SMARTDrive files.)

There are actually two different SMARTDrive device drivers you can use. DOS 5 ships with a file called SMARTDRV.SYS, which you load in your CONFIG.SYS file. DOS 6 and Windows ship with a different file, called SMARTDRV.EXE, which you load in your AUTOEXEC.BAT file. (If you're using DOS 5 with Windows, use SMARTDRV.EXE.)

Yikes!

Whichever file you use, be sure you're using the most recent version of SMARTDrive installed on your system. Because both DOS and Windows ship with SMARTDrive, you can end up with multiple versions on your hard disk. Use whichever SMARTDrive file that was installed with your most recent addition, whether this is DOS (or a DOS upgrade) or Windows. (The DOS and Windows SMARTDrive files are usually found in their respective directories.)

Creating a Disk Cache with SMARTDRV.EXE

If you're using Windows or DOS 6, the file for the device driver is SMARTDRV.EXE, which loads into your AUTOEXEC.BAT file. If you're using Windows with DOS 5 (or an earlier version), you should use the SMARTDRV.EXE file that shipped with Windows, which is normally installed in the WINDOWS directory. If you're using DOS 6 (with or without Windows), use the updated version of SMARTDRV.EXE, which is installed in the DOS directory. To load SMARTDRV.EXE, you need to add some variation of the following command line to your AUTOEXEC.BAT file:

```
SMARTDRV.EXE [InitCacheSize] [WinCacheSize]
```

As with the command to load a RAM disk (explained in Chapter 11, "What is a RAM Disk?"), this looks a little confusing, but it's really quite simple. You simply load the SMARTDRV.EXE file (from whichever directory it's located in), followed by the (optional) parameters shown in Table 12.1.

Table 12.1. SMARTDRV.EXE command parameters.

InitCacheSize	The size of the disk cache used for DOS-based applications, in K.
WinCacheSize	The size of the disk cache used for Windows, in K.

Skip This, It's Technical!

There are other parameters available for both SMARTDRV.EXE and SMARTDRV.SYS, but the ones I listed are the most useful—and the most commonly used. The other parameters available control things such as which drive is cached, the size of the read-ahead buffer (don't ask—it's *really* technical), and whether or not status messages are displayed when SMARTDrive is first loaded.

To determine the proper size cache for your setup, see Section III, "Easy Memory Setups Anyone Can Do," of this book. If you don't specify cache sizes, SMARTDRV.EXE estimates the amount of memory needed based on the free memory available. SMARTDRV.EXE automatically creates the disk cache in extended memory; you can't use SMARTDRV.EXE if you only have expanded memory.

If you want to create a disk cache of 2M for Windows use and 1M for DOS use, add the following line to your CONFIG.SYS file:

```
C:\WINDOWS\SMARTDRV.EXE 2048
```

Yikes!

Remember that 2M is not an even 2,000K, but actually 2,048K. Also, 1M is not 1,000K even, but rather 1,024K.

Creating a Disk Cache with SMARTDRV.SYS

If you're using the version of SMARTDrive that ships with DOS 5, the file for the device driver is SMARTDRV.SYS, which loads into your CONFIG.SYS file. To load SMARTDRV.SYS, you need to add some variation of the following command line to your CONFIG.SYS file:

```
DEVICE[HIGH]=C:\DOS\SMARTDRV.SYS [initialsize] [minsize] [/A]
```

As with the command to load SMARTDRV.EXE, this command is really quite simple. Simply use the `DEVICE` or `DEVICEHIGH` command (explained in Chapter 21, "Prepring for the Big Set Up") to load the SMARTDRV.SYS file from whichever directory it's located in (usually C:\DOS). You then can specify any of the parameters shown in Table 12.2.

Table 12.2. SMARTDRIVE.SYS command parameters.

`initialsize`	The size of the disk cache, in K. The default is 256K.
`minsize`	The minimum size of the cache if you're using Windows, in K. The default is 0.
`/A`	This switch places the disk cache in expanded memory.

If, for example, you have 2M of extended (not expanded) memory that you want to devote to a disk cache, and you're not running Windows (so you don't need to worry about minimum cache size), add the following line to your CONFIG.SYS file:

```
DEVICE=C:\DOS\SMARTDRV.SYS 2048
```

Using a Disk Cache

Using a cache drive is simple because it's invisible. The cache is created when your computer is first turned on, and it operates in the background without bothering you at all. DOS quietly loads data into the cache and reads it back as necessary—without your intervention. What could be simpler?

Should You Use a Disk Cache?

A disk cache is particularly valuable if you're using applications that frequently access your hard disk because it eliminates the need for DOS to continually read the same data from disk over and over again. Because most newer programs work this way (with a lot of hard disk reads), you're generally well-advised to use a disk cache.

If you're using Windows, you *must* use a disk cache—Windows just won't run well without it. Because SMARTDRV.EXE is optimized for Windows use, this is the cache driver of choice.

Skip This, It's Technical!

If you're running Windows, DOS 6 includes a special Windows utility called SMARTDrive Monitor that lets you observe how SMARTDrive is behaving. (You also can use it to change some of SMARTDrive's parameters.) To start SMARTDrive Monitor, pull down the File menu and select the Run option. When the Run dialog box appears, type `C:\DOS\SMARTMON`. From here you can do all sorts of super-technical disk caching stuff, if you're into that sort of thing.

You can use a disk cache and a RAM drive together without any problems. They both do their own thing and don't interfere with each other. Just remember that your memory is finite and exclusive—if you devote 1M to your RAM disk, that's 1M you can't use for your disk cache.

A disk cache differs significantly from a RAM disk (discussed in the preceding chapter). A RAM disk acts as a complete disk drive in memory, whereas a disk cache only holds in memory selected information from your existing hard disk. A RAM disk requires more management than a disk cache, and it is riskier to use—you can lose an entire "drive's" worth of information if your power goes off. A disk cache operates in the background without any attention from you, and it is less risky than a RAM drive.

Wrapping It All Up

I like disk caches much more than I like RAM disks. Disk caches are more reliable and easier to use than RAM disks, and they can really speed up your work! I heartily recommend that you create a disk cache if you have the free memory. You'll notice the increased performance immediately!

13

How Much Memory Do I Have On My Computer?

There are two main ways to find out about your system's memory using DOS commands. Both involve typing a command (with or without optional parameters)

at the DOS prompt. A readout on your screen then tells you either a little or a lot about your system's memory. (I suppose you could also take the top off your computer and count your memory chips, but who in the world would want to do that?)

Although the fastest and easiest ways to look at your system's memory involve DOS commands, there are also some ways to look at memory from within Windows. I'll discuss these methods later in this chapter.

Using the *CHKDSK* Command

If all you are interested in is your system's use of conventional memory (the first 640K of memory, as explained in Chapter 7, "What Different Kinds of Memory Are There?"), CHKDSK is the command for you. The CHKDSK command tells you how much conventional memory you have on your system and how much of it is currently free.

HMM...

CHKDSK also tells you all sorts of stuff about your hard disk, and it can also be used to find and fix lost chains of data on your hard disk. For now, however, I'll just concentrate on the memory aspects of CHKDSK.

To use CHKDSK, you have to issue the following command at the DOS prompt:

```
CHKDSK
```

Yikes!

Don't forget to press Enter after entering any DOS command!

When you initiate the CHKDSK command, DOS checks your system memory and provides an on-screen report like the one shown in Figure 13.1.

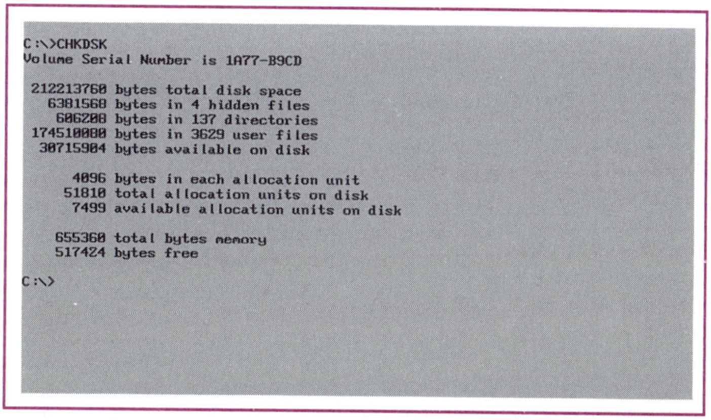

Figure 13.1. *The result of the CHKDSK command.*

For our purposes, you can ignore everything except the last two lines. (They deal with disk and file concerns, which are not relevant at the moment.)

The next-to-last line tells you how much conventional memory is present on your system. Note that it's not an even 640K; the extra bytes are there because of the way DOS counts things, and this is perfectly normal.

The last line tells you how many bytes are free—how much conventional memory is not currently being used by your system. (As you may recall from Chapter 7, conventional memory can be used by device drivers, terminate-and-stay-resident programs, and even DOS itself.)

The real value of CHKDSK is that it gives you a quick peek at how much conventional memory is available on your system. This is useful if you're trying to figure out if you have enough memory to load a particular program.

Using the *MEM* Command

If you want more detailed memory information, use the MEM command. MEM gives you a much more detailed report on your system's memory capacity and use.

PSST!

The MEM command is only available with DOS 4, 5, and 6. In fact, the screen display and operation of MEM is a little different between the older versions of DOS and DOS 6. In this book I'll show the DOS 6 operation, but DOS 4 and 5 operation is very similar.

To use MEM, you have to issue the following command at the DOS prompt:

```
MEM
```

Skip This, It's Technical!

MEM, like most DOS commands, has various parameters and options you can invoke when you issue the command. In MEM's case, the optional parameters let you display details about every little chunk of memory, including which programs are at which addresses. This information is really only of interest to real memory gurus, so just ignore it—you get more than enough information when you issue the plain, old MEM command!

When you initiate the MEM command, DOS checks all your system memory and provides an on-screen report. If you have DOS 6, the report looks like the one shown in Figure 13.2. If you have DOS 5, it looks like the one shown in Figure 13.3.

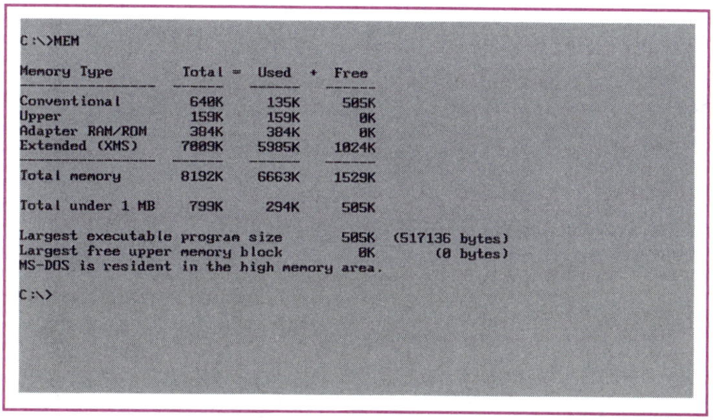

```
C:\>MEM

Memory Type        Total  =   Used   +   Free
----------------   -------   -------   -------
Conventional        640K      135K      505K
Upper               159K      159K        0K
Adapter RAM/ROM     384K      384K        0K
Extended (XMS)     7009K     5985K     1024K
----------------   -------   -------   -------
Total memory       8192K     6663K     1529K

Total under 1 MB    799K      294K      505K

Largest executable program size       505K  (517136 bytes)
Largest free upper memory block         0K       (0 bytes)
MS-DOS is resident in the high memory area.

C:\>
```

Figure 13.2. *The result of the MEM command in DOS 6.*

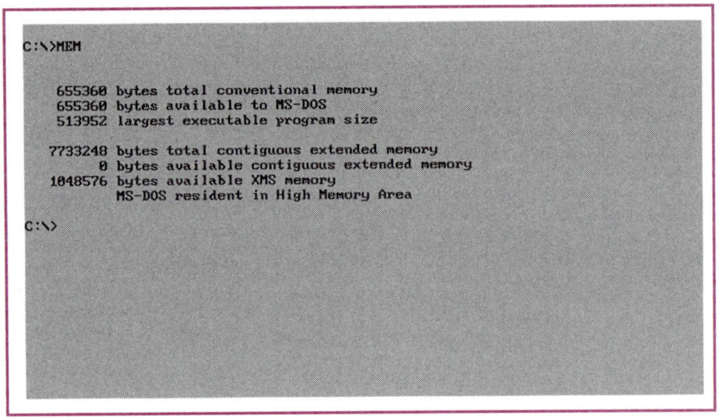

Figure 13.3. *The result of the* `MEM` *command in DOS 5.*

PSST! If you're using `MEM` in DOS 4 or 5, you'll immediately notice that the screen reports are quite different. The DOS 4/5 `MEM` report only gives you a brief summary of memory usage. If you're using DOS 4 or 5, you might want to issue the `MEM` command with the `/C` switch (like this: `MEM /C`), which gives you additional details of memory use.

`MEM` tells you a lot about your system's memory use. The four columns display the following information:

Memory Type — The type of memory on your system, including conventional, upper, extended, expanded, and so on.

Total — The total available memory for the type specified.

Used — The amount of memory currently in use for the type specified.

Free — The amount of free memory for the type specified

As you can probably figure out on your own, the total memory is equal to the memory used plus the free memory.

In this example, which is my personal system, I have four types of memory on my system: conventional, upper, extended (XMS), and *adapter RAM/ROM*, which is specific to my particular video card and reserved for video use. The `MEM` report for your system will probably look different from mine; you probably won't have the adapter RAM/ROM, and you may have expanded memory. In any case, whatever `MEM` reports is what you have!

After the memory type table, `MEM` lists the following information:

Total (memory) less than 1M	This is the amount of space in the conventional and upper memory areas.
Largest executable program size	This is the amount of space in conventional memory available to load programs into. (In my example, I have 505K free, which means I can load any program that requires 505K or less of memory.)
Largest free upper memory block	This is the size of the largest UMB into which drivers and so on can be loaded. (`MEM` reports that I have 0K free, which is actually good—I've maximized the use of UMBs on my system!)

Finally, `MEM` tells you if DOS is loaded into the high memory area (in my case, it is).

As you can see, the DOS 6 version of `MEM` gives you a lot of information about your system's memory usage. This is really the place to go when you need memory information.

Checking Your Memory in Windows

There really isn't an easy way to display memory usage from within Windows. Windows itself has no true memory reporting capabilities—about the best you can do is pull down the **H**elp menu in Program Manager and select the **A**bout Program Manager option. This displays the About Program Manager dialog box, which tells you in which mode you're running Windows, the amount of free *system resources* (a Windows-specific term that factors in several different parameters, including memory), and "memory." Note, however, that Windows counts temporary disk storage as "memory," so the figure displayed here is next to useless.

Although Windows itself is kind of useless when it comes to displaying memory information, certain third-party Windows utilities are available that do a better job. For example, Norton Desktop for Windows (my favorite Windows utility) has a module called System Information that can display some very detailed information about your system's memory from a Windows perspective (including exactly where in memory every single driver and interrupt is loaded).

When it comes right down to it, however, the best way to check your memory while in Windows is to open a DOS window and invoke the MEM command from the DOS prompt.

Wrapping It All Up

When you want to see how much memory is on your system—and how much is being used—the best way to go is to use the MEM command. Especially in DOS 6, MEM gives you all the information you need to make informed decisions about your system's memory use.

14

How Much Memory Do I Need?

As much as you can get (or afford)! Assuming you are not of unlimited means, however, I'll spend a few pages looking at memory needs for specific types of systems.

Memory Needs for a DOS System

The amount of memory you need if you're running DOS programs really depends on the programs you're running. Many DOS programs can't use extended or expanded memory, so anything above 1M goes unused.

PSST!

Even though many DOS programs can only use conventional memory, you can use upper memory to load device drivers, DOS itself, and so on. This means it's a good idea to have at least 1M of RAM, even if your programs can only use the first 640K.

If your programs can use extended or expanded memory, it's a good idea to check how much extra memory the publishers recommend for efficient use. If you're adding EMS or XMS, you can probably add it in 1M chunks. So if you add 1M for EMS, you have a total of 2M on your system (assuming it came with 1M standard). Table 14.1 contains different memory levels and the typical applications that can run efficiently within those memory levels.

Table 14.1. How much RAM do you need?

Total RAM	*Applications*
640K	Basic DOS operations, basic word processing (small documents), and basic PC games (few graphics).
1M	Normal word processing (medium-size documents), normal PC games (simple graphics), and basic spreadsheets (small files).

Total RAM	*Applications*
2M	Basic Windows operations (no multitasking), advanced word processing (large documents), advanced PC games (extensive graphics), normal spreadsheets (medium files), basic databases (small files), and basic presentation graphics (simple graphics).
4M	Normal Windows operations (multitasking, simple DDE operations), advanced spreadsheets (very large files, complex calculations), advanced database (large files), advanced presentation graphics (complex graphics), basic desktop publishing (simple documents), and basic drawings (simple drawings).
8M	Advanced Windows operations (advanced DDE and OLE operations), advanced desktop publishing (long, complex documents), and advanced drawings (complex, multilayered drawings).

Of course, even if your programs can't use EMS or XMS, you can use the added memory for disk caching or a RAM disk, both of which increase your system's performance.

Memory Needs for a Windows System

Chapter 15, "Do I Need More Memory If I Have Windows?" discusses Windows memory needs in more detail, but you need to know that Microsoft recommends a minimum of 2M RAM. My recommendation is to have at least 4M RAM for efficient Windows use.

Wrapping It All Up

This chapter should give you the idea that a 1M system just doesn't give you too many options. A 2M system is really the bare minimum you want for most purposes, and a 4M system should make you pretty comfortable. Naturally, if you can afford 8M or 16M (or even 32M or 64M), you're that much better off. So you're back to the original answer to the question—the right amount of memory is the most memory you can afford. It's really as simple as that!

15

Do I Need More Memory If I Have Windows?

Yes! Next question. . . .

Well, I suppose I should go into a little more detail about this scenario than just a simple, one-word answer. Let's look at why you need more memory if you have Windows.

Windows Needs Memory

Windows is a memory-intensive environment. Windows has to sit on top of DOS (that is, DOS itself is still running—and still loaded into memory), put some complex graphics on your screen (for that pretty graphical user interface), run some very large, memory-intensive programs (which also put lots of complex graphics on your screen), and then run *several* of these very large programs at the same time. It's tough to do that without a large amount of memory available.

Microsoft says Windows needs at least 2M of RAM to do its chores comfortably. I disagree with this. Although Windows might technically work with 2M RAM (by "work" I mean plodding along at the speed of a fully-loaded pack elephant), it really needs 4M to run well. Even with 4M, it's amazing that Windows can do all it does at an acceptable speed.

Skip This, It's Technical!

If you don't have enough memory available, Windows tries to use unused disk space as memory. This disk-space-as-memory method is called *virtual memory*, which can be assigned via the 386 Enhanced utility in the Windows Control Panel. Although this effectively gives Windows more "memory" to work with, hard disk access is so much slower than memory access that your system slows down noticeably when Windows has to use this virtual memory. You're better off adding as much real memory as possible to avoid the Windows virtual memory slowdown.

Some Windows programs add some strong demands on your system's memory. In particular, any program that creates really large or complex documents needs a lot of memory to do its job. These applications include the following:

- Long documents—50 pages or more—in word processors
- Large spreadsheets with complex calculations in spreadsheet programs
- Large files with complex graphics and lots of fonts in desktop publishing and presentation graphics programs
- Large databases with lots and lots of records

That said, it may be wise to check the memory requirements of your programs before you start them—you might find that they require more than the 2M minimum recommended by Microsoft.

In addition, some Windows operations require a substantial amount of memory to execute without crashing. In particular, *dynamic data exchange* (DDE) and *object linking and embedding* (OLE) require more than a few bytes of RAM to paste and link large amounts of data between different documents and programs. The RAM needs increase if you try to run multiple programs at one time (called *multitasking*). You may find that if you don't have enough memory, you're prohibited from fancy OLE use and you have to run your Windows applications one program at a time.

How Much Is Enough and How Much Is Too Much?

In my opinion, the bare minimum RAM you need to run Windows efficiently (and without undue risk of crashing) is 4M. With anything less, things get pretty slow and risky.

The fact of the matter is that lack of memory is the prime culprit for most mysterious Windows crashes (and the famous `Unrecoverable Application Error` and `General Protection Fault` error messages). My experience has shown that crash and error message rates decrease dramatically when you increase from 2M to 4M RAM—and almost completely disappear when you move to 8M! For these reasons, I recommend loading your machine with a minimum of 4M RAM if you're running Windows.

As to how much is too much, well, it's tough to say that you can have too much memory in Windows. However, if you're using Windows in a normal fashion (some multitasking, normal-sized word processing and spreadsheet documents, and so on), once you get above 8M you probably won't notice the difference.

However, if you're doing really fancy stuff (lots of complex graphics, large documents, extensive DDE and/or OLE use), then by all means add as much memory as you can afford. In fact, for heavy-duty desktop publishing/drawing operations, 16M might seem light. When in doubt, consult with the publishers of some of your most memory-intensive programs and see what they recommend.

Wrapping It All Up

Let's face it, Windows is a memory hog. It gobbles up extended memory like an elephant gobbles up peanuts. Unfortunately, memory costs more than peanuts, so you can't just add a bag of memory chips and be done with it. But if you have the bucks (and your system unit has the capacity), it certainly doesn't hurt to add as much memory as possible. Windows just plain runs better with more memory. Remember that and you'll do well.

16

How Do I Set Up My System for Maximum Memory Use?

To set up your system for maximum memory use, you first have to know what *to set up—and then you have to know* how *to set it up. Although these issues are* addressed in Section II, "Managing Your System's Memory," and Section III, "Easy Memory Setups Anyone Can Do," I'll give you a brief overview of what you'll get yourself into as you try to become a memory master!

Finding the Files to Fix

Most memory concerns are set when you turn your system on. You see, DOS reads two specific system files (CONFIG.SYS and AUTOEXEC.BAT) and relies on them for instructions on which device drivers to load and how to configure various system parameters.

This is where all the memory information gets fed into your computer—you really can't change anything once your computer is running. (This means you have to reboot your computer when you make any changes to these two files in order for the changes to take effect.)

Both CONFIG.SYS and AUTOEXEC.BAT are found in the root directory of your hard disk (usually C:\). Both files are ASCII text files, which means you can't save them in the same format you save your word processing documents. If you edit these files from your word processor, you have to save them in a special "Text" or "ASCII" format. It's easier, then, to use a text editing program that automatically reads and writes to this text format.

Using the DOS Editor

The most accessible text editor is the DOS Editor, which is included with DOS 5 and 6. (If you operate a previous version of DOS, you may want to use a third-party text editor, or chance it with your word processor and be sure you save in the right format.)

Launch the DOS Editor by typing (and then entering) the following line at the DOS prompt:

```
EDIT
```

Once the Editor is open, you can pull down the menus (either with a mouse or by pressing Alt to move the cursor to the menu bar) to access various editing commands. The command to Open files is found in the File menu; use this command to open the CONFIG.SYS and AUTOEXEC.BAT files. The File menu also contains the Save command, which you should use when you're done editing.

Editing CONFIG.SYS

CONFIG.SYS is actually the first file that DOS reads when it boots. DOS moves through CONFIG.SYS one line at a time, executing each line as a separate command. Among the memory-related commands and devices found in a typical CONFIG.SYS file are the following:

- *HIMEM.SYS*
- *SMARTDRV.SYS*
- *RAMDRIVE.SYS*
- *EMM386.EXE*
- *BUFFERS*
- *FILES*

Yikes!

The order in which these devices are loaded and in which the commands are executed is important. Putting things in the wrong order can actually decrease the amount of free memory available! See Chapter 21, "Managing Your System's Memory," for more details on how to set up your CONFIG.SYS file for maximum memory use.

Editing AUTOEXEC.BAT

AUTOEXEC.BAT is the second file DOS reads when it boots. As it does with the CONFIG.SYS file, DOS moves through AUTOEXEC.BAT one line at a time, executing each line as a separate command. The most common memory-related command found in a typical AUTOEXEC.BAT file is SMARTDRV.EXE.

Making the Most of What's There

Once you figure out *what* to set up (the CONFIG.SYS and AUTOEXEC.BAT files), you need to know *how* to set them up. All the commands and devices impact how your system's memory is used—in particular, what types of memory are activated and what is supposed to be loaded where.

Conventional Memory

The best way to maximize conventional memory is to move as much stuff as possible out of it! That's right, you really want to free up as much conventional memory as possible for your programs to use. So any chance you have to move a device driver or a small program into another level of memory, do it!

Upper Memory

Upper memory blocks (UMBs) are great for loading device drivers and small programs that might otherwise occupy conventional memory space. The best scenario is if you can fill all your UMBs. There's nothing more satisfying than running the MEM command and finding that you have 0 free UMB space, which means you did a great job of maximizing upper memory use!

The High Memory Area

The high memory area (HMA) is the first 640K of extended memory. Unfortunately, you can't access the HMA without loading a special device driver called HIMEM.SYS. When this driver is loaded, the HMA can be filled with device drivers (or DOS itself) or used as part of extended memory. The bottom line with the HMA is to use it in whatever way makes best sense.

Extended and Expanded Memory

If you have more than 1M memory, you have either extended (XMS) or expanded (EMS) memory. (The more memory the merrier!)

Which should you use, extended or expanded? If you're only running DOS programs—and those programs can use expanded memory—then EMS is the way to go. If you're running Windows, however—or running any DOS programs that use extended memory—then go with XMS.

PSST!

Remember, you need to load an EMS or XMS manager to use this extra memory. The XMS manager included with DOS is called EMM386.EXE, and it is loaded via the CONFIG.SYS file.

If you're running only DOS programs, you may want to create a disk cache and/or a RAM disk. These are great ways to use the XMS or EMS that might not otherwise be used by many DOS programs.

If you're running Windows, you want to free up as much extended memory as possible. This means keeping RAM disks and disk caches to a minimum—leave as much as you can for Windows. My recommendation is to create a small disk cache (no more than 25 percent of your available XMS), forget about the RAM disk, and leave the rest for Windows.

However you do it, be sure your extra memory is being used. There's nothing more frustrating than seeing a 4M system with everything crammed into the first 640K and all the extra memory sitting unused. Don't waste your chips—use as much memory as you can!

Wrapping It All Up

This chapter was really a condensed version of the material found in Sections II and III of this book. The chapters in those sections address the different ways you can set up your system (depending on the makeup of your system). Start reading at Chapter 22, for a much more detailed examination of what was briefly covered here.

17

Which Version of DOS Is the Best for Memory Management?

The answer is DOS 6, no doubt about it. If you want to know why DOS 6 is so good, read on.

DOS 6 Is Good

You would probably expect the latest version of DOS to be the best version. After all, things are supposed to improve with age (except for that month-old carton of milk in the refrigerator, that is). And DOS, like most things, has gotten better with each revision.

DOS 6 includes all the memory management tools you need to get the most from your system's memory. In previous versions of DOS, there always seemed to be one or more things lacking—things that were readily available in third-party, memory-management software programs. Prior to DOS 6, if you wanted to do everything you could do with your memory, you had to buy a third-party program—with that attendant cost and bother. But with DOS 6, you finally get everything you need self-contained in the operating system.

PSST! 

If you want to get the real low-down on all the new features of DOS 6, pick up a copy of a really good book from Sams, *DOS Secrets Unleashed*, by well-known author Alan Simpson. This book is a great guide to all the features of DOS 6, and it includes a ton of tips and tricks to get the most out of your operating system.

The best thing about DOS 6 is a little utility program called MEMMAKER. This wonderful little program essentially sets up your system for maximum memory use—automatically! That's right, with MEMMAKER, you probably won't have to edit a single CONFIG.SYS or AUTOEXEC.BAT file. Run MEMMAKER once, and your system is set for life. (In previous versions of DOS you had to figure out the most effective settings for all your options and then make the changes yourself. What a bother!)

DOS 6 also includes memory managers (EMM386.EXE and HIMEM.SYS), disk caching (SMARTDRV.EXE), a RAM disk (RAMDRIVE.SYS), and a memory report generator (MEM.EXE). Put all this together, and you get a very efficient system for managing your system's memory.

DOS 5 Is Okay

DOS 5 includes most of the memory management features included in DOS 6, although it doesn't include MEMMAKER. This means you can get pretty much the same memory maximization as with DOS 6, but it's just a little harder to do so. You have to edit your CONFIG.SYS and AUTOEXEC.BAT files yourself and figure out how they should be edited.

Skip This, It's Technical!

There are some other small differences between DOS 5 and DOS 6. DOS 5 uses SMARTDRV.SYS instead of SMARTDRV.EXE, and the DOS 5 version of MEM generates reports that are less detailed than those in DOS 6.

Of course, with the help of the advice in this book, you should know most of what you need to do to maximize your memory. So if you don't mind doing some of the work yourself, DOS 5 is okay for memory management, but DOS 6 is better!

Other DOSs Aren't That Hot

None of the versions of DOS prior to DOS 5 were all that hot in terms of memory management. DOS 4 and preceding versions just didn't have the right tools to make memory management easy—in fact, they didn't even have memory managers like HIMEM.SYS and EMM386.EXE! That's right, prior to DOS 5, you were pretty much forced to buy a third-party, memory-management package if you wanted to use anything beyond the first 640K of conventional memory. So if you have DOS 4 or an earlier version, upgrade to DOS 6 immediately! Okay?

Wrapping It All Up

Table 17.1 outlines the memory management features of the different versions of DOS.

Table 17.1. DOS memory management features.

Feature	*DOS 6*	*DOS 5*	*DOS 4*	*DOS 3.3 (and earlier versions)*
MEM	Yes	Yes (limited)	Yes (limited)	No
MEMMAKER	Yes	No	No	No
SMARTDRV.EXE	Yes	No	No	No
SMARTDRV.SYS	No	Yes	No	No
EMM386.EXE	Yes	Yes	No	No
HIMEM.SYS	Yes	Yes	No	No
RAMDRIVE.SYS	Yes	Yes	No	No

There you have it. Primarily due to the ease of use of MEMMAKER, DOS 6 is really the way to go in terms of memory management. So if you have an older version of DOS (especially if it's DOS 4 or earlier), run—don't walk—to your local software emporium, pull out some bills or a charge card, and grab a copy of the DOS 6 upgrade. You'll find it's money very well spent!

18

Should I Use Another Memory Manager?

The answer to this question really depends on the version of DOS you're using and the programs you're trying to run. So, let's take a look at the whole subject of memory managers, focusing on third-party solutions.

Why You Would Want Another Memory Manager

The memory management available in DOS 6 is great—especially if you have an 80386- or 80486-based computer. But if you have an older computer using 8088/8086 or 80286 chips, there are some areas of memory (such as upper memory blocks) that DOS 6 can't access. Most third-party memory managers do a better job with older computers than does DOS; if you have an older computer, you should consider a third-party program.

If you have a version of DOS prior to DOS 5, third-party memory management is just plain better than what's built into the operating system. DOS 4 and earlier versions did not manage memory well. If you have one of these older operating systems, you either need to upgrade to DOS 6 or use a third-party memory management solution.

If you're using some older DOS programs that use expanded memory (EMS), you should also consider a third-party solution. DOS just isn't optimized for expanded memory—about the best it can do is configure itself to use extended memory as expanded memory. If you're serious about expanded memory, invest in an EMS card with a corresponding EMS memory manager.

Finally, you may just dislike the way DOS handles memory management (or how Microsoft handles MS-DOS) and choose a third-party solution out of spite. That's okay with me; to each his or her own!

What's Available

There are a lot of third-party memory-management programs available. I'll list the most popular programs (in alphabetical order), along with a brief description of what they do and why you might want to use them.

386MAX

386MAX is a memory manager for 80386-based PCs from Qualitas. This program comes with a memory manager, RAM disk and disk cache drivers, and various memory-management utilities. 386MAX is capable of loading various device drivers and TSR programs into UMBs and operates automatically (like MEMMAKER in DOS 6).

BlueMAX

BlueMAX from Qualitas is a version of 386MAX developed specifically for IBM PS/2 computers (80386-based). It functions almost identically to 386MAX.

MOVE'EM

MOVE'EM is another program from Qualitas, developed specifically for 8088/8086- and 80286-based PCs. It works in conjunction with EMS memory and lets you load device drivers and TSRs into UMBs, all somewhat automatically.

QEMM-386

QEMM-386 is a memory manager for 80386- and 80486-based PCs from Quarterdeck. This program includes Manifest, a first-rate system evaluation program more advanced than DOS's MEM command. Many users find QEMM-386 more efficient in using upper memory space than DOS's EMM386.EXE memory manager. In addition, the Optimize utility completely automates memory setup.

QRAM

QRAM is another Quarterdeck program developed specifically for 8088/8086- and 80286-based PCs. It works in conjunction with EMS memory and includes the Manifest evaluation program.

PSST!

Although the focus of this book is on MS-DOS, there's an alternative version of DOS available from Novell called DR DOS. DR DOS isn't a memory manager per se, but rather a replacement operating system for MS-DOS that includes its own memory management devices and commands. If you're using DR DOS, you have to learn a whole new set of commands and drivers to manage your memory—but all in all, memory management with DR DOS is very similar to that in MS-DOS.

Wrapping It All Up

Table 18.1 contains a list of the most popular third-party memory managers and the systems to which they are best suited.

Table 18.1. Third-party memory managers.

System	*386MAX*	*BlueMAX*	*MOVE'EM*	*QEMM-386*	*QRAM*
8088/8086	No	No	Yes	No	Yes
80286	No	No	Yes	No	Yes
80386	Yes	Yes*	No	Yes	No
80486	Yes	Yes*	No	Yes	No
PS/2	No	Yes	No	No	No

*only for PS/2-based systems

If you have an older 8088/8086- or 80286-based computer, you want either MOVE'EM or QRAM. If you have an 80386- or 80486-based IBM-compatible PC, 386MAX or QEMM-386 are the ones for you. If you're using an IBM PS/2, BlueMAX is the only program optimized for your system.

However, if you're using DOS 6, you probably don't have much to gain by switching to a third-party memory manager. If you have a prior version of DOS, your money is better spent on the DOS 6 upgrade than it is on a third-party program. (Are you starting to get the impression that I think DOS 6 has pretty good memory-management capabilities?)

19

How Do I Add More Memory?

There are really two key ways to add more memory to your system. One way, if you're a klutz like me, is to take your PC into your local computer shop and pay them to do it for you. (This is preferable to trying to figure out the cryptic markings on the side of your chips to determine their capacity and adding up all the bits and bytes to make sure you have the right amount of RAM in the right place.) The other way is to open up the system unit and plug in new chips or boards all by yourself. You should judge your own level of technical competence to determine which method is best for you.

What Kind of Memory Should You Add?

There's a little bit you need to know about memory chips before you plunk down your hard-earned cash, so let's take a look at the types of things you should be looking for. Of course, I still recommend calling in a pro for a lot of this stuff; at the very least, you need someone to check what kind of memory you have in your system and recommend the right RAM to add.

PSST!  If you really want detailed information about adding memory to your system, skip ahead to Chapter 26, "Adding Memory to Your System."

Choosing the Right Chip

As explained in Chapter 3, "Where Is My System's Memory?" most PCs use dynamic RAM (DRAM) chips. You can get various kinds of chips (see Table 19.1).

Table 19.1. Types of memory chips.

Type	*Function*
DIP	*Dual in-line package.* This chip is a flat rectangle with 16 metal legs, and it kind of looks like a spider. DIPs plug into little sockets on your motherboard.
SIMM	*Single in-line memory module.* A SIMM is kind of like a miniature expansion card, a few inches long, that has nine RAM chips presoldered to the card. A SIMM doesn't have legs, it has an edge connector, and it slides into a SIMM socket on your motherboard.
SIP	*Single in-line package.* A SIP is a long, multichip chip, kind of like a SIMM. The big difference between a SIMM and a SIP is that a SIP has a single row of legs instead of an edge connector.
ZIP	*Zigzag in-line package.* A ZIP is a SIP with two rows of legs, staggered on the same edge of the chip.

DIPs are the most common types of DRAM chips, and often the least expensive. The kind of chip you buy depends on what your system uses, plain and simple.

If you're adding expanded memory (EMS), you don't add individual chips, you add an *expanded memory card.* (Some cards come empty and you have to add chips to them.) The card should come with an EMS driver to manage your system's use of the expanded memory.

Choosing the Right Speed

There are three characteristics that affect the chip's speed (see Table 19.2).

Table 19.2. Memory chip speed factors.

Factor	*Description*
Access time	The amount of time it takes to access one bit of data, measured in nanoseconds (ns). The lower the number, the better; 80 ns is faster than 120 ns, for example.
Wait state	The number of clock cycles that your CPU must sit through while a RAM chip stores one number and prepares to store another. (This is called a *refresh cycle*.) The lower the number, the better; 0 wait states is better than 2 wait states.
Interleaving	This term refers to how memory addresses are assigned. Noninterleaved memory uses sequential addresses; interleaved memory divides memory into odd and even numbered addresses. In essence, it's like having one tall stack of blocks versus two shorter stacks—it's easier to get to the top with shorter stacks. Therefore, it's easier to find a particular memory address with interleaved memory.

Choosing the Right Size

You can generally get DRAM chips in one of three common sizes: 64Kb, 256Kb, or 1Mb. The size you use is determined by your system. Most systems require you to add chips of a specified size. And, no, you can't put a 1Mb chip in a socket designed for a 64K chip!

Yikes!

If you're adding multiple chips (which you probably are), be sure all the chips are of the same brand. Mixing and matching chips from different manufacturers can sometimes cause memory problems!

DRAM chips contain bits of memory, not bytes. (This is why they're labeled as Kb instead of K.) So if you want to add 1M (megabyte) of memory, you need to add up enough bits to get there. For example, it takes eight 1Mb chips to get 1M of RAM, since there are 8 bits in a byte. (Actually, when you buy memory chips, you get them in banks of nine. The extra chip is necessary for "parity bits"—a concept that goes way beyond the scope of this book.) Table 19.3 gives you an idea of how different RAM chips add up.

Table 19.3. Adding up the RAM.

Chip	*# for 1M*	*# for 2M*	*# for 3M*	*# for 4M*
64Kb	144	288	432	576
256Kb	36	72	108	144
1Mb	9	18	27	36

Of course, you're not going to add over 500 chips to your motherboard! Instead, you want to use the larger 1Mb chips—or a SIMM that includes multiple chips on a single module.

Skip This, It's Technical!

When you add new chips (or assess your current system's memory) you need to figure out the capacity of each chip. You can use the part number of most chips (stamped on the top of the chip) to figure out the RAM capacity and access time. Normally, the last three or four digits of the part number indicate the chip's capacity—a chip labeled 41256 is a 256Kb chip, for example. The access time is normally part of a dash following the part number—if you see 41256-80, the chip has an 80 ns access time.

Choosing the Right Type of Memory

The type of memory you add to your system depends on your system itself (see Table 19.4).

Table 19.4. The right type of memory.

System	*Options*
8088/8086	Conventional memory, expanded memory card
80286	Conventional memory, extended memory, expanded memory card
80386	Conventional memory, extended memory, expanded memory card
80486	Conventional memory, extended memory, expanded memory card

Although you can add an expanded memory card to any system, you have to have an 80286 or better CPU to add extended memory.

Putting All the Chips in Place

Installing chips isn't as hard as it might seem. You need to take certain precautions and take extreme care, but it really comes down to a matter of plugging chips into sockets.

First, you need to turn off (and unplug) your system unit. Open the case of the system unit and identify the position of your RAM chip sockets. Most PCs have at least one bank of sockets (in sets of 9, 18, or 36) to hold RAM chips. As explained in Chapter 3, there is no set position for your chip banks. It's a good idea to consult the schematic of your PC (normally included with the instruction manual) to locate your RAM banks.

Yikes!

Static electricity can destroy RAM chips. Be sure you discharge any static electricity from your body before touching any RAM chips. You can do this by touching something metal, such as your computer's case. Some pros even wear antistatic bracelets to prevent static buildup while they are working on PCs. Above all, don't shuffle your feet on the carpet (or rub a balloon on your sweater) in the middle of RAM installation!

Orient the chip so that all the legs are lined up with the corresponding holes on the socket. When each leg is lined up properly, press firmly but gently on the chip to seat it into the socket. Voila! The chip is inserted!

After you're done installing all your memory, you need to reset some options on your system and software so that it recognizes your additional memory. Consult your PC's instruction manual on how to access the setup program to reconfigure your system's memory settings.

PSST!  You can also add memory via a memory expansion card. Most cards come without RAM chips installed—you have to buy RAM chips separately. You should plug the chips into the card first and then plug the card into your system unit.

Wrapping It All Up

Well, I still prefer the "let someone else do it" answer to this question, but adding memory isn't one of the hardest things you can do to your system. It doesn't hurt to consult with a pro, however, or have a phone number handy if you get into trouble with the case off. However you add your memory, though, you'll be glad you did—with additional memory, your system works a whole lot better than it ever did before!

20

What Can Go Wrong with My System's Memory?

Let's take a page or two to examine just what kinds of problems you can look forward to when dealing with your system's memory (and believe me, there are lots of potential problems).

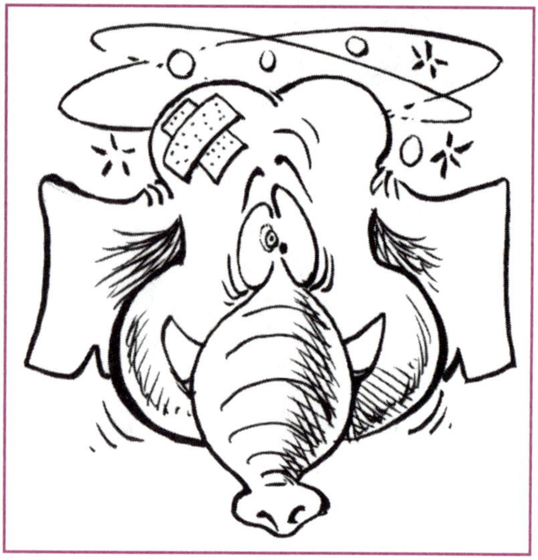

Common Problems

Most memory problems are caused by incorrect setups. That is, the instructions imparted via the CONFIG.SYS and AUTOEXEC.BAT files aren't the right ones for your particular setup. You may try to load something into high memory when there is no high memory available, or you may load your devices in the wrong order. Whatever the case, you need to get these files in order if you want your system to work right!

Order is important. You need to load certain devices before you can load other devices. For example, before you can load anything into UMBs, you need to activate extended memory with HIMEM.SYS and open upper memory with EMM386.EXE. If these two lines aren't the first two lines in your CONFIG.SYS file, you won't be able to load anything into UMBs—no matter what commands you enter!

Sometimes you can load devices into high or extended memory that don't belong there. I've had my system lock up when I tried to load certain device drivers into UMBs. For some reason, some drivers just won't go where you want them to go.

Another common problem is using the wrong device driver. You always want to use the latest version of any driver. For example, both Windows 3.1 and DOS 6 come with SMARTDRV.EXE files. Use the one that came with DOS 6; it's the latest version, and it works better. (Updated drivers often include fixes for bugs found in older versions!)

If you're adding new memory to your system, you can experience lots of problems if you don't tell your system about the new memory. You need to run your PC's setup program to reconfigure it for the additional memory. You may also need to flip some DIP switches on your motherboard to recognize the new memory. Of course, if you inserted the RAM chips (or expansion card) incorrectly, you'll also have problems.

Yikes!

While you're configuring things, don't forget to reconfigure your software programs to take advantage of the additional memory available.

It's also possible to get hold of bad RAM chips. You may need to do some plugging and replugging to figure out which chips are bad and which are good. (If things start working right after you remove a chip, the chip is probably bad.) While you're checking your chips, be sure they are plugged in securely. (This also applies if you're using a memory expansion card—except in this case, check both the chip connections and the card itself!)

Common Solutions

Because most problems are caused by incorrect CONFIG.SYS and AUTOEXEC.BAT files, let's focus on fixing them.

Yikes!

It's a good idea to create an emergency boot disk so you can reboot your system from a floppy disk in case things get so bad your system won't even start. See Chapter 21, "Preparing for the Big Setup," for instructions.

First things first—always make a backup of these system files before you start messing with them! This way you can revert to the backup copies if you really screw things up.

Now you need to examine your files line by line. If you're loading things above 640K, bring them all back into conventional memory. (This means changing the `LOADHIGH` and `DEVICEHIGH` commands to normal `LOAD` and `DEVICE` commands—see Chapter 21). Now restore the high loading instructions, one line at a time, always saving the file and rebooting your system between changes. In this way, you should be able to isolate the line that's causing all your problems.

Yikes!

Remember that you need to reboot your system for any changes you make to CONFIG.SYS and AUTOEXEC.BAT to take place.

If you're using DOS 6, the easiest solution is to simply use MEMMAKER to fix things for you automatically. (See Chapter 23, "Working With DOS 6 Memory Management Tools," for details on using MEMMAKER.)

Yikes!

Of course, it's possible for MEMMAKER to make mistakes. You may need to manually adjust certain settings after MEMMAKER is done.

If you're using one or more terminate-and-stay-resident programs, you may need to take them out of memory. (Most TSRs are loaded via commands in the AUTOEXEC.BAT file.) TSRs can cause a lot of memory problems, and if you can find a way not to use them, you're probably better off.

If all else fails, consult with someone who knows more than you do about fixing PC problems. After all, that's what the pros get paid for! (I consider using computer repair shops my way of supporting the service economy.)

Wrapping It All Up

The scary thing about memory problems is that they often cause your computer to completely lock up, forcing you to reboot—on many occasions from your emergency boot disk. Fortunately, most memory problems are easy to fix, even though they may take a bit of time to track down. Have patience, though—once you locate that one line that's causing your problems, it won't take more than a minute to correct the culprit.

Part II

Managing Your System's Memory

In Section I, "Twenty Questions About Memory Management," you learned the least of what you need to know about what memory is and how it works. In this section I get down to the nitty-gritty details of how you actually change your memory setup—how you edit your system files, how you use the DOS 6 memory management tools, how you manage Windows memory, and how you add more memory to your system. If you already know how to do these things, feel free to skip to Section III, "Easy Memory Setups Anyone Can Do," for detailed instructions on how your system should be set up. Otherwise, turn the page and read on!

21

Preparing for the Big Setup

Well, after reading through the twenty questions in Section I, "Twenty Questions About Memory Management," you know a little bit about how memory works. Now let's roll up our sleeves and figure out how to implement changes to your system to maximize your memory use.

Before you start messing around with things, however, there are a few items you need to prepare—just in case something goes wrong (I'm not saying it will, but hey, you never know, right?).

Creating an Emergency Boot Disk

If things really get messed up with your setup, you may not even be able to start your computer. To prepare for this possibility, you need to devise a way to start your computer without all the changes you've made to your setup files.

What Goes On When the Light Goes On

Fortunately, your computer always goes through a systematic set of operations when you turn it on. After your computer's BIOS is activated, your PC goes looking for a copy of DOS. The first place it looks is in your A: drive; if no disk is in the drive, it looks on your hard drive (usually drive C:). So, under normal circumstances (i.e., no disk in drive A:), your computer finds DOS on your hard drive, executes the CONFIG.SYS and AUTOEXEC.BAT files, and waits for you to do something.

If your CONFIG.SYS or AUTOEXEC.BAT files are messed up, it can completely hang your computer. You need to bypass these files to get your computer to start—just so you can make the necessary changes to the messed-up files!

This is where the A: drive booting comes in. If you have a "bootable" disk in drive A: (that is, a disk that contains the DOS system files), your computer boots from the A: drive, never accessing the messed-up files on drive C:.

The Emergency Boot Disk—Step by Step

You need to prepare a disk that you can use to boot your system in an emergency—the emergency boot disk. To prepare the emergency boot disk, grab a blank disk, stick it in drive A:, and follow these instructions:

1. From the C: prompt, format the disk in drive A: as a *system disk* by typing the following command:

   ```
   FORMAT A: /S
   ```

> **Skip This, It's Technical!**
>
> The /S switch in the FORMAT command copies necessary "hidden" system files to the disk. Without these files, the disk wouldn't boot!

2. When the formatting is complete, copy your CONFIG.SYS file to the disk by typing the following command:

   ```
   COPY C:\CONFIG.SYS A:
   ```

3. Now copy your AUTOEXEC.BAT file to the disk by typing the following command:

   ```
   COPY C:\AUTOEXEC.BAT A:
   ```

4. When you're done, remove the disk from the drive, label it "emergency boot disk," and put it away in a safe (but convenient) place.

Yikes!

Never—and I repeat, *never*—try to format your hard disk! This means you should never type the command `FORMAT C:`! If you do, all the information on your hard disk will be lost—this is probably not what you had in mind!

Using the Emergency Boot Disk in an Emergency

Whenever you have trouble starting your system normally (due to changes you've made to CONFIG.SYS or AUTOEXEC.BAT), all you have to do is insert the emergency boot disk into drive A: and then reboot your computer. When your system comes back up, it reads your old files from the disk in drive A:, thus bypassing any errors you introduced to the system files on your hard disk.

Now you can change to your hard disk and edit the files in question. (Just remember to remove the disk from drive A: after you correct the problems in your hard disk files!)

Backing Up Your System Files

There's one more precaution you should take before you start editing your system files: make backup copies of your original files on your hard disk. (Yeah, I know that you'll keep backups on your emergency boot disk, but you may still be able to boot your PC, and it's easier to copy files to and from a single hard drive.)

To make backup copies of these files with the ORG extension (for "original"), type the following commands at the C: prompt:

```
COPY C:\CONFIG.SYS C:\CONFIG.ORG
COPY C:\AUTOEXEC.BAT C:\AUTOEXEC.ORG
```

If you ever completely mess up your main files and want to revert to the saved versions, all you have to do is reverse the commands:

```
COPY C:\CONFIG.ORG C:\CONFIG.SYS
COPY C:\AUTOEXEC.ORG C:\AUTOEXEC.BAT
```

Yikes!

When you copy the .ORG files over the main .SYS and .BAT files, you're totally erasing the bad files. You may wish to save these files under different extensions before they're copied over. This way you can examine the files to figure out what was causing the problem at hand.

Editing CONFIG.SYS and AUTOEXEC.BAT with the DOS Editor

I've talked a lot about editing your system files. Well, just how do you go about doing that? If you have DOS 5 or 6, you have a utility program called the DOS Editor. This program is a text editor, which is nothing more or less than a very simple word processor. The DOS Editor saves files in what is called the ASCII text format; not coincidentally, this is the same format used by DOS to read your system files.

PSST! If you have an older version of DOS, or just don't like the DOS Editor, you can use any word processor to edit these system files. Just be sure to save the files in the ASCII text format (normally an option with the program's Save As command). Whatever you do, don't save your CONFIG.SYS and AUTOEXEC.BAT files in the native file format for your word processor—DOS won't be able to read them at all!

Launching the DOS Editor

You start the DOS Editor by typing the following command at the DOS prompt:

```
EDIT
```

The DOS Editor, as shown in Figure 21.1, now appears. Press Esc to remove the opening dialog box.

As you can see, the DOS Editor looks like a typical word processor, complete with pull-down menus. You can access these menus with your mouse, or by hitting the Alt key.

Once your cursor is on the menu bar, you can use the right and left arrow keys to move from one menu to another or just type the first letter of any menu option. Then use the down arrow key to pull down the desired menu and move to the desired menu option. When you've selected the desired menu option, press Enter to execute that option.

Opening a File

To open the CONFIG.SYS file, follow these steps:

1. Press Alt+F to pull down the File menu.

2. When the Open dialog box appears (see Figure 21.2), type the following line in the File Name box:

   `C:\CONFIG.SYS`

3. Click on the OK button or press the Enter key.

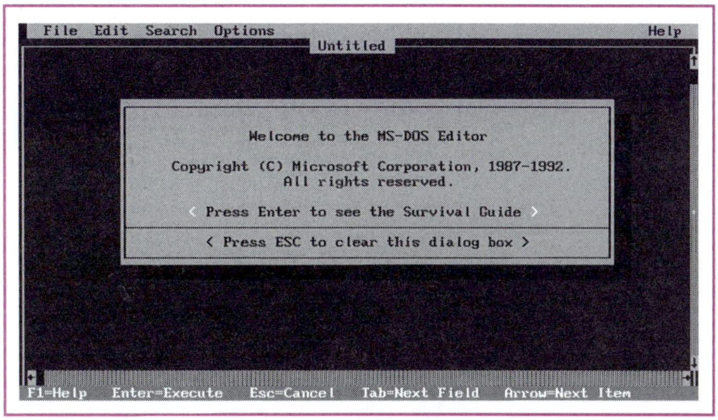

Figure 21.1.
The DOS Editor.

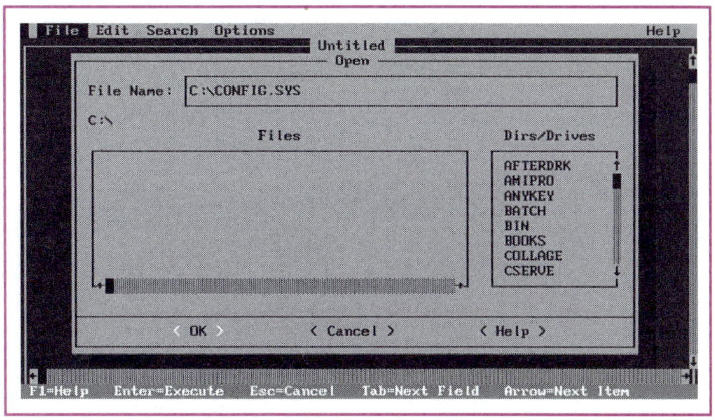

Figure 21.2.
The Open dialog box in the DOS Editor.

PSST! Follow the same steps to open AUTOEXEC.BAT, although you should type this line into the File Name box:

```
C:\AUTOEXEC.BAT
```

After the CONFIG.SYS file is loaded, a screen that looks like the one shown in Figure 21.3 appears. Each line represents a separate command. (I'll get into more detail on these commands later in this chapter.) Your screen probably looks different from the one in Figure 21.3 because every system has unique aspects that require a slightly different setup.

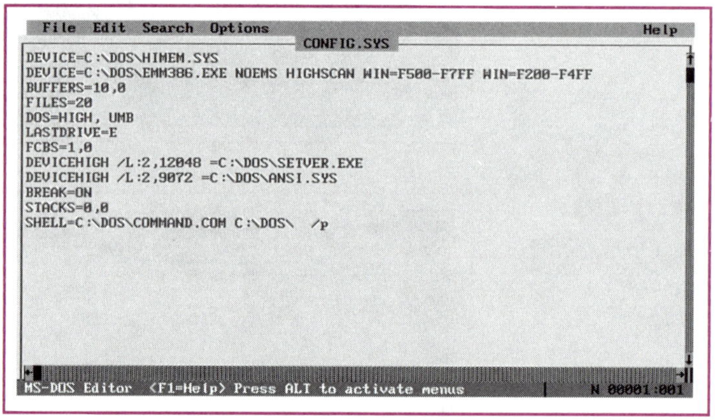

Figure 21.3. *A typical CONFIG.SYS file shown in the DOS Editor.*

Editing a File

There are numerous editing functions available with the DOS Editor. Most are available via the Edit menu, from which you can cut, copy, and paste text to and from different sections of your file (or even between files). It's also pretty easy to just move the cursor anywhere in the file and insert new text or delete old (using either the Backspace or Delete keys) text.

Saving and Closing

When you're done editing and want to save the file, follow these steps:

1. Press Alt+F to pull down the File menu.
2. Press S to Save the file.

To close the file and exit the DOS Editor, follow these steps:

1. Press Alt+F to pull down the File menu.
2. Press X to Exit the DOS Editor.

As you start experimenting with your CONFIG.SYS and AUTOEXEC.BAT setups, you'll become very familiar with the DOS Editor—trust me.

Checking Your Work with *MEM*

As you make changes to your system, you may want to measure the impact of your changes on your system's memory use. The easiest way to do this is with the MEM command.

To use MEM, type the following at the DOS prompt:

```
MEM
```

When you initiate the MEM command, DOS checks all your system memory and provides an on-screen report. If you have DOS 6, the report looks like the one shown in Figure 21.4.

The MEM report for your system will probably look different from mine—each system's memory use is different.

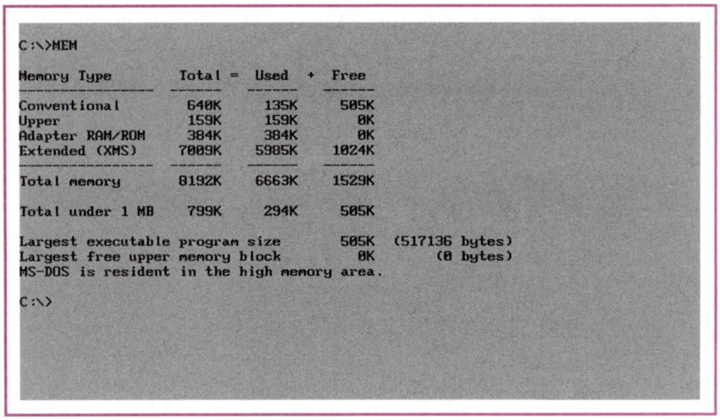

```
C:\>MEM

Memory Type        Total  =  Used  +  Free
----------------  -------   ------   ------
Conventional        640K     135K     505K
Upper               159K     159K       0K
Adapter RAM/ROM     384K     384K       0K
Extended (XMS)     7009K    5985K    1024K
----------------  -------   ------   ------
Total memory       8192K    6663K    1529K

Total under 1 MB    799K     294K     505K

Largest executable program size      505K  (517136 bytes)
Largest free upper memory block        0K       (0 bytes)
MS-DOS is resident in the high memory area.

C:\>
```

Figure 21.4.
The result of the MEM command in DOS 6.

PSST!

The screen reports generated by versions of MEM prior to DOS 6 are quite different and less informative. If you're using DOS 4 or 5, you might want to issue the MEM command with the /C switch (MEM /C), which gives you additional details of your memory use. The /C switch is discussed later in this section.

What *MEM* Tells You

MEM tells you a lot about your system's memory use, including the information shown in Table 21.1.

Table 21.1. MEM information.

Memory Type	The type of memory on your system, including conventional, upper, extended, expanded, and so on.
Total	The total available memory for the type specified.

Used	The amount of memory currently in use for the type specified.
Free	The amount of free memory for the type specified.
Total (memory) less than 1M	The amount of space in the conventional and upper memory areas.
Largest executable program size	The amount of space in conventional memory available to load programs into.
Largest free upper memory block	The size of the largest UMB into which drivers and so on can be loaded.

Finally, MEM tells you if DOS is loaded into the high memory area.

Even More *MEM*

If you want even more information about what exactly is loaded into memory—and where—there are optional parameters you can add when issuing the MEM command. The most useful parameter is the /C switch, which gives you a complete list of all programs and drivers in memory.

PSST!

If you use the /C switch, you probably also want to use the /P switch, which tells MEM to display the report one page at a time. Otherwise, the entire report scrolls past your eyes so fast you won't even know what's happening.

When you use MEM with the /C switch, you get one or more screens that look like those shown in Figures 21.5 and 21.6.

Figure 21.5.
Page one of the DOS 6 MEM report with the /C switch activated.

```
Modules using memory below 1 MB:

  Name           Total       =   Conventional   +   Upper Memory
  --------  ----------------   ----------------   ----------------
  MSDOS       11645    (11K)     11645    (11K)          0    (0K)
  HIMEM        1168     (1K)      1168     (1K)          0    (0K)
  EMM386       3120     (3K)      3120     (3K)          0    (0K)
  COMMAND      2912     (3K)      2912     (3K)          0    (0K)
  SAVE        72624    (71K)     72624    (71K)          0    (0K)
  MOUSE       17088    (17K)         0     (0K)      17088   (17K)
  SMARTDRV    28816    (28K)         0     (0K)      28816   (28K)
  AD-DOS       5040     (5K)         0     (0K)       5040    (5K)
  SETVER        832     (1K)         0     (0K)        832    (1K)
  ANSI         4240     (4K)         0     (0K)       4240    (4K)
  Free       670544   (655K)    563664   (550K)     106880  (104K)

Memory Summary:

  Type of Memory       Total       =      Used       +      Free
  ----------------  ----------------   ----------------   ----------------
  Conventional       655360   (640K)     91696    (90K)    563664   (550K)
  Upper              162896   (159K)     56016    (55K)    106880   (104K)
  Adapter RAM/ROM    393216   (384K)    393216   (384K)         0     (0K)
Press any key to continue . . .
```

Figure 21.6.
Page two of the DOS 6 MEM report with the /C switch activated.

```
  SMARTDRV    28816    (28K)         0     (0K)      28816   (28K)
  AD-DOS       5040     (5K)         0     (0K)       5040    (5K)
  SETVER        832     (1K)         0     (0K)        832    (1K)
  ANSI         4240     (4K)         0     (0K)       4240    (4K)
  Free       670544   (655K)    563664   (550K)     106880  (104K)

Memory Summary:

  Type of Memory       Total       =      Used       +      Free
  ----------------  ----------------   ----------------   ----------------
  Conventional       655360   (640K)     91696    (90K)    563664   (550K)
  Upper              162896   (159K)     56016    (55K)    106880   (104K)
  Adapter RAM/ROM    393216   (384K)    393216   (384K)         0     (0K)
Press any key to continue . . .
  Extended (XMS)    7177136  (7009K)   2323376  (2269K)   4853760  (4740K)
  ----------------  ----------------   ----------------   ----------------
  Total memory      8388608  (8192K)   2864304  (2797K)   5524304  (5395K)

  Total under 1 MB   818256   (799K)    147712   (144K)    670544   (655K)

  Largest executable program size       563568   (550K)
  Largest free upper memory block        99216    (97K)
  MS-DOS is resident in the high memory area.

C:\>
```

As you can see, every single item that is loaded into memory is listed, along with the type of memory it's using—and how much. The format of the report is similar to that of the regular MEM report, you just have a lot more information listed.

The /C version of MEM is very useful for determining which driver is loaded where. It helps you track down items that might not be loaded where they ought to be.

Wrapping It All Up

Well there, you needed to know all that before you start getting your hands dirty with essential memory management stuff. You would be surprised how often you need to edit your system files, or check into what's really in your memory with MEM. And, unfortunately, things blow up often enough that the emergency boot disk is not only good insurance, it's often a life saver!

But enough of these preliminaries, it's time to turn the page and start setting up your system for some efficient memory use!

22

Setting Up Your System for Maximum Memory Use

Now it's time to move beyond the preliminaries and get down to the real stuff. Over the next few pages I'll examine strategies for maximizing each kind of

memory on your system. The goal is to free up as much conventional memory as possible by loading drivers and programs into nonconventional memory.

This chapter assumes that you're using DOS 5 or 6 without any external memory managers. It also assumes that you have at least 1M of RAM on your system.

Using High Memory

Before you can use any memory above 640K on your system, you need to activate the high memory area (HMA), which is the first 64K of extended memory. To activate the HMA, you have to load a high memory manager. The high memory manager included with DOS is called HIMEM.SYS, and it is loaded via the CONFIG.SYS file.

Skip This, It's Technical!

You have to have HIMEM.SYS loaded before you can access extended memory as well. This means you have to load HIMEM.SYS before EMM386.EXE in your CONFIG.SYS file.

Loading HIMEM.SYS

To load HIMEM.SYS, add the following line at the very beginning of your CONFIG.SYS file:

```
DEVICE=C:\DOS\HIMEM.SYS
```

Yikes!

If you're using a version of HIMEM.SYS that resides in another directory (such as the one that comes with Windows), substitute that directory for the DOS directory in the preceding command.

When HIMEM.SYS is loaded, you should see the following line in your `MEM /C` report:

Name	*Total*	=	*Conventional*	+	*Upper Memory*
HIMEM	1168 (1K)		1168 (1K)		0 (0K)

Loading DOS High

Once HIMEM.SYS is activated, you can load one other important item into the HMA—DOS itself! You load DOS into HMA by adding the following command to your CONFIG.SYS file:

```
DOS=HIGH
```

When DOS is loaded in the HMA, you should see the following line at the end of your `MEM` report:

```
MS-DOS is resident in the high memory area.
```

Using Upper Memory Blocks

Because most computers come with at least 1M of memory and programs can only use the first 640K of this memory, it makes sense to use that memory between 640K and 1M, which is called the upper memory area. This memory is divided into blocks, called upper memory blocks (UMBs). You can only load items into UMBs if the HMA is activated, so you need to be sure HIMEM.SYS is loaded before proceeding.

Loading EMM386.EXE

You need to load the EMM386.EXE memory manager before you can use UMBs. EMM386.EXE fills UMBs with memory (as well as activating extended or expanded memory). You activate EMM386.EXE by including the following command in your CONFIG.SYS file:

```
DEVICE=C:\DOS\EMM386.EXE NOEMS
```

Yikes!

This command should be the second line in your CONFIG.SYS file (right after your HIMEM.SYS line).

Creating UMBs with the DOS Command

You also need to create some UMBs before you load them. You do this via the `DOS` command in your CONFIG.SYS file. As you may recall, you also used this command to load DOS into HMA. Now you need to add an additional parameter to this command to create UMBs in upper memory. You do this by editing the command in CONFIG.SYS to look like the following:

```
DOS=HIGH,UMB
```

Yikes!

The `DOS` command must be located in CONFIG.SYS after the EMM386.EXE line and before any `DEVICEHIGH` commands.

Loading Devices into Upper Memory with *DEVICEHIGH*

Items that are generally loaded into conventional memory are prime candidates to move into UMBs. Normally you load devices in your

CONFIG.SYS file via the `DEVICE` command. For example, you would normally load the ANSI.SYS device driver with the following command:

```
DEVICE=C:\DOS\ANSI.SYS
```

To load a driver into UMBs, use the `DEVICEHIGH` command instead of the normal `DEVICE` command. To load ANSI.SYS in UMBs, then, place the following command in your CONFIG.SYS file:

```
DEVICEHIGH=C:\DOS\ANSI.SYS
```

Yikes!

The `DEVICEHIGH` command must replace the existing `DEVICE` command—you can't load the same device twice!

When a driver is loaded into UMBs, `MEM` reports it as part of upper memory, as in the following example:

Name	*Total*	=	*Conventional*	+	*Upper Memory*
ANSI	4240 (4K)		0 (0K)		4240 (4K)

Loading Devices into Upper Memory with *LOADHIGH*

You can also load devices via commands in the AUTOEXEC.BAT file. In this file, devices are normally loaded just by their filename (because they must be executable files with an .EXE extension). For example, to load the MSMOUSE.EXE driver, you would normally include a line like the following:

```
C:\MOUSE\MSMOUSE.EXE
```

If you want to load this driver into UMBs, you have to use the `LOADHIGH` command. So, to load MSMOUSE.EXE into UMBs, replace the existing command in AUTOEXEC.BAT with the following line:

```
LOADHIGH C:\MOUSE\MSMOUSE.EXE
```

Skip This, It's Technical!

You can also use the `LH` command, which is a shortened version of `LOADHIGH`.

To ensure that the driver has been loaded into UMBs, check your `MEM` report to see if the device is using upper memory, as in the following example:

Name	*Total*	=	*Conventional*	+	*Upper Memory*
MSMOUSE	17088(17K)	0	(0K)		17088 (17K)

Using Extended Memory

If you already loaded EMM386.EXE, you activated your system's extended memory. You see, in addition to activating your system's upper memory, EMM386.EXE is your system's extended memory manager. (This driver can also function as an expanded memory manager, as explained in the next section.)

So, if you want to activate your extended memory—and you don't intend to use any expanded memory—add the following line as the second line in your CONFIG.SYS file:

```
DEVICE=C:\DOS\EMM386.EXE NOEMS
```

The NOEMS parameter tells EMM386.EXE not to simulate expanded memory (EMS). You'll want to change this parameter if you're using EMS, as explained in the next section.

Once extended memory is activated, you can use it with programs that use XMS (such as Windows) and use it to store disk caches and RAM disks.

Using Expanded Memory

Expanded memory is used with many older DOS programs; it is not used with Windows or Windows applications. You activate expanded memory via the EMM386.EXE memory manager.

All you have to do is change the NOEMS parameter to the RAM parameter. This tells EMM386.EXE to create expanded memory out of your extra RAM. You can also specify the amount of RAM (in K) devoted to EMS; the default setting is 256K.

If you want to create a 1M expanded memory area, the command you add to CONFIG.SYS looks like this:

```
DEVICE=C:\DOS\EMM386.EXE 1024 RAM
```

Once extended memory is activated, you can use it with programs that use EMS and use it to store disk caches and RAM disks.

Dealing with Files and Buffers and Things

There are other commands in your CONFIG.SYS file that affect memory usage. Table 22.1 lists these items, along with recommended minimum values (to maximize free conventional memory), and a brief description of what they do.

Table 22.1. Other commands.

Command	*Minimum Value*	*Description*
BUFFERS	10,0	Creates a set number of disk buffers in memory that temporarily hold disk data in memory. If you're using SMARTDrive, you can set this command value very low because SMARTDrive is doing the buffering; 10 is the recommended minimum.
FILES	20	Specifies the number of files that DOS can access at one time. Although the default value is 8, if you're using Windows, you need to set it a little higher; 20 is a good compromise.
FCBS	1,0	Specifies the number of file control blocks (FCBs) that DOS can have open at one time. If you're on a network, use 4 as the value; if you're not networked, use 1.
STACKS	0,0	Specifies how much memory to reserve for processing hardware interrupts. Although some sources recommend setting stacks at 9,256, I've found that 0,0 works just as well—and it saves a lot of memory!

A system using the minimum values for each of these commands would include the following lines in the CONFIG.SYS file:

```
BUFFERS=10,0
FILES=20
FCBS=1,0
STACKS=0,0
```

Adding a Disk Cache

The smartest use of additional memory is the use of a disk cache. A disk cache acts like a buffer for important data; all information read from your hard disk is copied to the disk cache. When DOS needs that data again, it accesses the cache, which is must faster than a normal hard disk access.

Using SMARTDRV.EXE with DOS 6

With DOS 6 (or with Windows) you create a disk cache by loading the SMARTDRV.EXE driver via your AUTOEXEC.BAT file. To load SMARTDRV.EXE, you need to add some variation of the following command line to your AUTOEXEC.BAT file:

```
SMARTDRV.EXE [InitCacheSize] [WinCacheSize]
```

The optional parameters are shown in Table 22.2.

Table 22.2. SMARTDRV.EXE parameters.

`InitCacheSize`	The size of the disk cache used for DOS-based applications, in K.
`WinCacheSize`	The size of the disk cache used for Windows, in K.

PSST!

If you don't specify cache sizes, SMARTDRV.EXE estimates the amount of memory needed based on the free memory available.

You can also load SMARTDRV.EXE into UMBs using the `LOADHIGH` command. If you want to create a disk cache of 2M for Windows use and 1M for DOS use, add the following line to your CONFIG.SYS file:

```
LOADHIGH C:\DOS\SMARTDRV.EXE 2048 1024
```

PSST! SMARTDRV.EXE automatically creates the disk cache in extended memory; you can't use SMARTDRV.EXE if you only have expanded memory.

Skip This, It's Technical!

There is an option to SMARTDRV.EXE called *double buffering* that you may need to use with certain hard disks that cannot work with EMM386.EXE. To use SMARTDRV.EXE's double-buffering, you need to add the following command to your CONFIG.SYS file:

```
DEVICE=C:\DOS\SMARTDRV.EXE /DOUBLE_BUFFER
```

You still need to load the normal SMARTDRV.EXE in your AUTOEXEC.BAT file. Most hard disks don't require double buffering; this is really something for rare occasions.

Using SMARTDRV.SYS with DOS 5

If you're using DOS 5 (without Windows) you create a disk cache by loading the SMARTDRV.SYS driver via your CONFIG.SYS file. To load SMARTDRV.SYS, you need to add some variation of the following command line to your CONFIG.SYS file:

```
DEVICE[HIGH]=C:\DOS\SMARTDRV.SYS [initialsize] [minsize] [/A]
```

The optional parameters are shown in Table 22.3.

Table 22.3. SMARTDRV.SYS Parameters.

`initialsize`	The size of the disk cache in K. The default is 256K.
`minsize`	The minimum size of the cache if you're using Windows in K. The default is 0.
`/A`	This switch places the disk cache in expanded memory.

If you want to create a 2M disk cache in extended memory (and load the SMARTDRV.SYS driver into UMBs), add the following line to your CONFIG.SYS file:

```
DEVICEHIGH=C:\DOS\SMARTDRV.SYS 2048
```

If you want to create the same disk cache in expanded memory, add this line to CONFIG.SYS:

```
DEVICEHIGH=C:\DOS\SMARTDRV.SYS 2048 /A
```

Adding a RAM Disk

A RAM disk is a *virtual* disk drive—that is, it's memory that your system *thinks* is a real disk drive. DOS lets you read and write to a RAM disk just like you would a normal hard disk. But because your RAM disk is in memory, you can access it much faster than you can a normal hard disk.

Yikes!

A RAM disk is as volatile as anything else in RAM. The RAM disk only exists while the power is on—if you experience a sudden power outage, all the data currently stored on the RAM disk is lost.

If you're using DOS 5 or 6, you create a RAM disk by loading the RAMDRIVE.SYS driver via your CONFIG.SYS file. To load this driver, add some variation of the following command line to your CONFIG.SYS file:

```
DEVICE[HIGH]=C:\DOS\RAMDRIVE.SYS [disksize] [sectorsize]
[direntries] [/E] [/A]
```

The optional parameters are shown in Table 22.4.

Table 22.4. RAMDRIVE.SYS parameters.

`disksize`	The size of the RAM disk in K. The default is 64K.
`sectorsize`	The size of the sectors used for the RAM disk in bytes. The default is 512 bytes.
`direntries`	This puts a limit on the number of files and directories that can exist in the root directory of the RAM disk. The default is 64.
`/E`	This switch places the RAM disk in extended memory.
`/A`	This switch places the RAM disk in expanded memory. (If you don't use either switch, the RAM disk is placed in conventional memory.)

If you want to create a 2M RAM disk in extended memory (using default values, but loading the RAMDRIVE.SYS driver into UMBs), add the following line to your CONFIG.SYS file:

```
DEVICEHIGH=C:\DOS\RAMDRIVE.SYS 2048 /E
```

To create the same RAM disk in expanded memory, add this line to CONFIG.SYS:

```
DEVICEHIGH=C:\DOS\RAMDRIVE.SYS 2048 /A
```

Wrapping It All Up

Whew! That's a lot of information for one chapter. But you now know everything you need to know to edit your CONFIG.SYS and AUTOEXEC.BAT files for maximum memory usage.

If you're using DOS 6, however, there is an easier way to maximize your memory management—and it's called MEMMAKER. Turn the page to find out more about making DOS 6 memory management much easier!

23

Working with DOS 6 Memory Management Tools

Before we go on, be sure you've read Chapter 22, "Setting Up Your System for Maximum Memory Use." Although DOS 6 can do a lot of things automatically, it

still helps to have a firm background of what it's doing, which you can get from the previous chapter.

Well, now that that's out of the way, let's look at specific features of DOS 6 that can make your memory management a more manageable task.

All About MEMMAKER

MEMMAKER is a new utility that ships with DOS 6. If you don't have DOS 6, you don't have MEMMAKER. (This is reason enough to go out and purchase the DOS 6 upgrade!)

What It Is and What It Does

MEMMAKER is a program that runs from the DOS prompt. It automatically determines your system setup and makes changes to your CONFIG.SYS and AUTOEXEC.BAT files to maximize your system's use of memory. MEMMAKER loads as many devices as possible into upper memory to free up conventional memory for normal program use. It also maximizes the use of upper memory by specifying specific addresses for your drivers (something you could do if you knew as much about your system as MEMMAKER does), thus packing things together in a highly efficient manner.

Skip This, It's Technical!

When you examine your CONFIG.SYS and AUTOEXEC.BAT files after MEMMAKER has reconfigured your system, you may notice that many of your commands are much longer and contain many more parameters. For example, what was once a simple `DEVICEHIGH=C:\DOS\ANSI.SYS` may turn into something a tad more cryptic:

```
DEVICEHIGH /L:2,9072=C:\DOS=ANSI.SY
```

In my particular setup, my `DEVICE=C:\DOS\EMM386.EXE NOEMS` line had a bunch of confusing parameters tacked on at the end:

```
DEVICE=C:\DOS\EMM386.EXE EMS HIGHSCAN WIN=F500-F7FF
WIN=F200-F4FF
```

In each case, these are parameters I could have added on my own had I known enough about how my system works and where exactly each device was stored. Because MEMMAKER scans your entire memory in immaculate detail, it can specify exact addresses in which to load each of your drivers. This is one reason to run MEMMAKER at least once on your system—there's no way you can specify this kind of detail on your own.

When You Should and Shouldn't Use It

You should use MEMMAKER whenever you want to maximize your system's memory. This means you should run it when you first set up your computer, after you change operating systems (like upgrading to DOS 6), and after you add new programs or devices to your system. Using MEMMAKER is infinitely preferable to making all these changes yourself—even if you could figure out exactly what changes need to be made!

You may not want to run MEMMAKER if you're using only Windows and Windows applications. You see, MEMMAKER uses little chunks of extended memory to free up more conventional memory, and Windows needs all the extended memory it can get. However, I still recommend you run MEMMAKER if you're running Windows. It does such an efficient job, you can easily edit any mistakes it makes (in regard to Windows use) afterward.

Running MEMMAKER

Running MEMMAKER is easy. Just type the following command at the DOS prompt:

```
MEMMAKER
```

Yikes!

You have to run MEMMAKER from the DOS prompt. You can't run it from within Windows or from the DOS Shell. You also should close any currently running programs before starting MEMMAKER.

When MEMMAKER starts, you're presented with the screen shown in Figure 23.1.

Press Enter to move to the next screen, which gives you a choice of setups: Express or Custom. For most users, Express Setup is the right way to go. It's easy and requires virtually no input on your part. If you fancy yourself more of a memory management guru, however, you should choose Custom Setup. Custom gives you more options to choose from and makes you feel like you're really contributing to the process. It's possible that you might squeeze a few more bytes of memory out of Custom Setup, but I still think Express is the way to go.

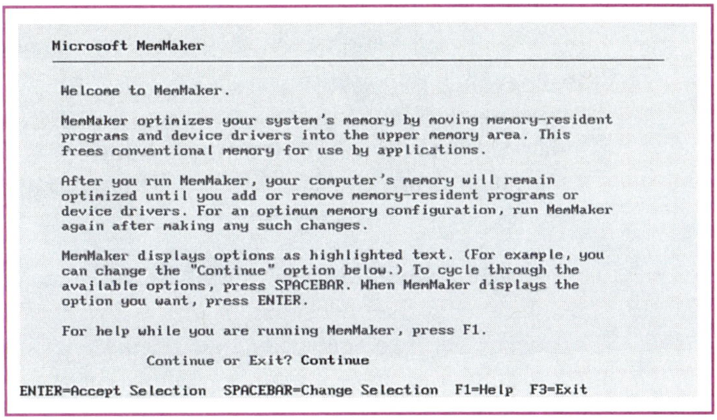

Figure 23.1. *The initial MEMMAKER screen.*

PSST!

You can switch between options in MEMMAKER by pressing the spacebar, which kind of acts like a toggle switch, toggling between all the available options.

Running the Express Setup

When you first enter MEMMAKER's Express Setup, you're asked if you use any programs that require expanded memory (EMS). After you answer Yes or No, Express Setup goes into action, checking your system setup. If it finds a copy of Windows installed, it asks you for some information about where Windows is installed. Answer the questions and let MEMMAKER do some more work.

After a few moments, MEMMAKER displays a screen stating that it will now restart your computer. Press Enter to continue with the MEMMAKER setup or Esc to cancel the setup.

MEMMAKER now reboots your PC. As your computer restarts, MEMMAKER takes note of each line in your CONFIG.SYS and

AUTOEXEC.BAT files as they're executed, analyzing how each command uses memory. MEMMAKER then uses this analysis to determine the optimum memory setup for your computer, which means choosing from thousands of possible configurations. When the best setup is determined, MEMMAKER rewrites your CONFIG.SYS and AUTOEXEC.BAT files and asks for your okay to reboot your system once more.

When you press Enter, MEMMAKER reboots your system again, this time with the new setup in place. If your system is working properly, you're all set and can exit MEMMAKER at the proper prompt. If your system isn't working right, you need to tell MEMMAKER so when prompted; MEMMAKER will then try some more options for your setup.

Yikes!

It's about impossible to screw up MEMMAKER. If it has trouble rebooting after changing your system configuration, it simply resets things, starts again, and lets you know what's happening. Pretty foolproof, if you ask me.

Running the Custom Setup

If you choose to run MEMMAKER's Custom Setup, you're first prompted if you use any programs that require expanded memory (EMS). After you answer Yes or No, Custom Setup displays the Advanced Options screen, as shown in Figure 23.2.

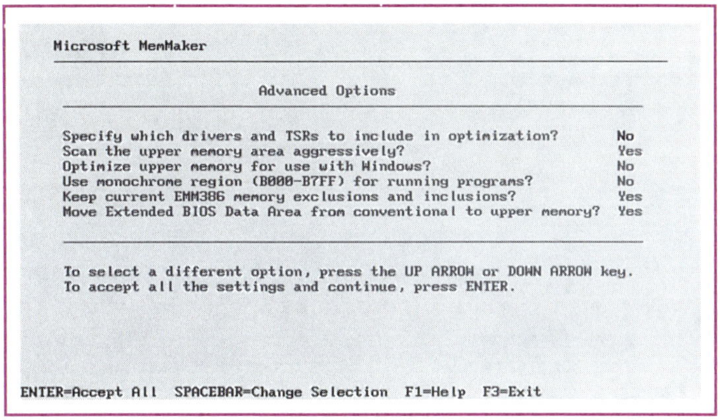

Figure 23.2. *MEMMAKER's Advanced Options screen.*

The options on this screen include:

Specify which drivers and TSRs to include in optimization? Unless you specify otherwise, MEMMAKER includes all device drivers and TSRs in the optimization process. If a particular program causes problems when running MEMMAKER, you may need to tell MEMMAKER to leave it out of the optimization process.

Scan the upper memory area aggressively? You should enter Yes to this, unless you've run into problems when using MEMMAKER.

Optimize upper memory for use with Windows? This is a little confusing, and it involves how MEMMAKER optimizes things. In general, it tries to push as much stuff as possible into extended memory to free up conventional memory. However, Windows really doesn't use that much conventional memory, preferring to use as much extended

	memory as possible. Anyway, answer Yes if you run DOS programs from within Windows (or just by themselves); answer No if you run only Windows and Windows applications.
Use monochrome region (B000-BFFF) for running programs?	This can free up some otherwise unused memory for other items. Answer Yes if you use an EGA or VGA monitor. Answer No if you use a SuperVGA or monochrome monitor.
Keep current EMS386 memory exclusions and inclusions?	Answer Yes only if you had trouble running MEMMAKER previously. Answering No allows MEMMAKER to change some settings for a more efficient memory configuration.
Move Extended BIOS Data Area from conventional to upper memory?	This moves some DOS BIOS data into upper memory, freeing up additional conventional memory. Answer Yes to move the BIOS; answer No only if you had trouble running MEMMAKER previously.

Change any of these settings as appropriate, then press Enter to continue. The Custom Setup now goes into action. If it finds a copy of Windows installed, it asks you for some information about where Windows is installed. Answer the questions and let MEMMAKER do some more work.

Yikes!

You need to know that when you start messing with the options available in Custom Setup—and you don't know what you're doing—you increase the chances of MEMMAKER actually doing more harm than good and locking up on the reboot. So, if you're uncomfortable with the Custom Setup options, revert to the Express Setup and save yourself some headaches!

After a few moments, MEMMAKER displays a screen stating that it will now restart your computer. Press Enter to continue with the MEMMAKER setup or Esc to cancel the setup.

MEMMAKER now reboots your PC. As your computer restarts, MEMMAKER analyzes how each command in your system files uses memory. MEMMAKER then determines the optimum memory setup for your computer, rewrites your CONFIG.SYS and AUTOEXEC.BAT files, and asks for your okay to reboot your system once more.

When you press Enter, MEMMAKER reboots your system again, this time with the new setup in place. If your system is working properly, you're all set, and you can exit MEMMAKER at the proper prompt.

Cleaning Up After MEMMAKER

Believe it or not, MEMMAKER isn't perfect. You may wish to edit its recommended configuration for even better management, or you may wish to throw out everything it did and start from scratch. I'll show you how to do each if you can hang on for another page or so.

Customizing Your Setup

Now, as good as MEMMAKER is, there are times when you can do even better. You may find that you want some drivers loaded into conventional memory instead of upper memory to free up more space for other things. Or you may find that you can free up a tad more memory by changing the order in which you load your drivers. Whatever the reason, you want to make some changes to MEMMAKER's "perfect" setup.

Well, making changes is easy—in fact, you learned how to do it in Chapter 22! That's right, after you let MEMMAKER do all the hard work, you can now open up your CONFIG.SYS and AUTOEXEC.BAT files and tweak your setup till the cows come home. While it's unlikely you'll do any better than MEMMAKER did, you never know, do you?

Undoing MEMMAKER's Changes

If you absolutely despise MEMMAKER's setup and want to restore your system to the state it was in before MEMMAKER, all you have to do is type the following command at the DOS prompt:

```
MEMMAKER /UNDO
```

MEMMAKER then restores your original CONFIG.SYS and AUTOEXEC.BAT files, and you're back where you started from.

Wrapping It All Up

Well, it took quite a few pages to tell you how to do something that's basically very easy. To sum up, when you want to maximize your memory under DOS 6, type MEMMAKER at the DOS prompt, choose Express setup, and sit back while MEMMAKER does all the work. Pretty neat, eh?

24

Using Third-Party Memory Managers

As discussed way back in Chapter 18, "Should I Use Another Memory Manager?" there are times when you may want to use a third-party memory manager. For example, third-party solutions make sense if you fall into any of the following categories:

- You are using an 8088/8086-based computer.
- You are using an 80286-based computer.
- You are using a version of DOS prior to DOS 5.
- You are using some older DOS programs that use expanded memory (EMS).

If any of these situations apply to you, read on and I'll talk about basic features and operations of some of the more popular third-party memory managers.

Yikes!

If you decide to use a third-party memory manager, read the instructions very carefully. You'll find that you need to delete some DOS commands from your system files, or things won't work at all!

You'll also want to use the device drivers and loading commands specific to your memory manager, instead of the normal DOS drivers and commands. (For example, with 386MAX, you use 386LOAD.SYS instead of `DEVICEHIGH` in your CONFIG.SYS file.) I've noted some of the important driver/command changes for each of the major third-party memory managers.

Using 386MAX and BlueMAX

386MAX is a memory manager from Qualitas designed for 80386- and 80486-based systems (BlueMAX is the PS/2 version of 386MAX and has nearly identical operation). Both programs include the following features:

- A RAM disk.

- Disk caching.
- The ability to turn unused areas of upper memory into UMBs.
- The ability to convert extended memory into expanded memory on a real-time basis.
- The ability to use the first chunk of upper memory as conventional memory.
- Squeeze, a utility that "shrinks" TSRs and other small programs after installation, freeing additional upper memory.
- ASQ, a utility that analyzes your system's memory usage (similar but superior to MEM).

386MAX is simple to install via its built-in Install program. This program installs all the 386MAX programs and utilities on your hard disk.

To maximize memory usage, run the Maximize program (similar to MEMMAKER) from the DOS prompt. This program optimizes your system, making changes to your CONFIG.SYS and AUTOEXEC.BAT files as necessary.

Yikes!

If you're using 386MAX, BlueMAX, or MOVE'EM with DOS 5 or 6, you need to eliminate the DOS=UMB command from your CONFIG.SYS file, or else you won't be able to load anything into upper memory!

386MAX uses its own versions of similar DOS device drivers (see Table 24.1).

You'll want to substitute the 386MAX device drivers for the DOS device drivers in your system files.

Table 24.1. Equivalent 386MAX device drivers.

386MAX Version	*DOS Version*
386MAX.SYS	HIMEM.SYS/EMM386.EXE
386LOAD.SYS	`DEVICEHIGH`
386LOAD.COM	`LOADHIGH`

All in all, 386MAX and BlueMAX (for IBM PS/2 computers) are programs that give you efficient memory management in a very easy-to-use fashion.

> HMM... When you purchase 386MAX, you get a copy of MOVE'EM at no charge.

Using MOVE'EM

MOVE'EM is a memory manager from Qualitas designed for 8088/8086- and 80286-based systems. It works exclusively with expanded memory and includes the following features:

- The ability to load TSRs and device drivers into upper memory.
- The ability to load DOS resources into upper memory.
- An upper memory manager to create UMBs.

MOVE'EM also installs via an Install program that copies all relevant programs and utilities to your hard disk. However, MOVE'EM lacks an optimization program like Maximize or MEMMAKER, so you have to edit all your system files manually.

MOVE'EM uses its own versions of similar DOS device drivers (see Table 24.2).

You'll want to substitute the MOVE'EM device drivers for the DOS device drivers in your system files.

Table 24.2. MOVE'EM device drivers.

MOVE'EM Version	*DOS Version*
MOVE'EM.MGR	HIMEM.SYS/EMM386.EXE
MOVE'EM.SYS	`DEVICEHIGH`
MOVE'EM.COM	`LOADHIGH`

If you have an older computer and an EMS memory card, MOVE'EM is a good way to manage your expanded memory.

Using QEMM-386

QEMM-386 is a memory manager from Quarterdeck designed for 80386- and 80486-based systems. It includes the following features:

- "Stealth" technology that turns unused areas of upper memory into UMBs.
- The ability to "spool" extended memory into expanded memory on a real-time basis.
- DOS Resource Programs that load FILES, BUFFERS, FCBS, and LASTDRIVE into upper memory.

- Manifest, a topnotch utility that analyzes your system's memory usage (similar but superior to `MEM`).
- Optimize, a utility that determines the best order for loading TSRs and device drivers into upper memory.
- VIDRAM, a utility that uses the first chunk of upper memory as conventional memory.
- Squeeze, a utility that "shrinks" TSRs and other small programs after installation, freeing additional upper memory.
- QEMM386.SYS, a single device driver that replaces both EMM386.EXE and HIMEM.SYS.

Like the other programs listed, QEMM-386's Install program installs all the programs and utilities to your hard disk. You then use the Optimize program (similar to MEMMAKER) to optimize your memory management. Optimize analyzes your system and makes the appropriate changes to your CONFIG.SYS and AUTOEXEC.BAT files.

Skip This, It's Technical!

Even if you're using QEMM-386, it's still a good idea to include the `DOS=HIGH` statement in your CONFIG.SYS file to free up additional conventional memory.

QEMM-386 uses its own versions of similar DOS device drivers (see Table 24.3).

You'll want to substitute the QEMM-386 device drivers for the DOS device drivers in your system files.

Table 24.3. QEMM-386 device drivers.

QEMM-386 Version	*DOS Version*
QEMM386.SYS	HIMEM.SYS/EMM386.EXE
LOADHI.SYS	`DEVICEHIGH`
LOADHI.COM	`LOADHIGH`

Like 386MAX, QEMM-386 is a program that gives you efficient memory management in a very easy-to-use fashion.

Using QRAM

QRAM is a memory manager from Quarterdeck designed for 8088/8086- and 80286-based systems. It works exclusively with expanded memory, and includes the following features:

- The ability to load TSRs and device drivers into upper memory.
- The ability to load DOS resources into upper memory.
- An upper memory manager to create UMBs.
- Optimize, a utility that determines the best order for loading TSRs and device drivers into upper memory.
- VIDRAM, a utility that uses the first chunk of upper memory as conventional memory.

Skip This, It's Technical!

VIDRAM essentially steals the video RAM used by your video card and glues it onto conventional memory, giving you more than 640K conventional memory for program use.

QRAM's installation program automatically copies all programs and utilities to your hard disk. You then use the Optimize program (the same one used in QEMM-386) to optimize your memory management. Optimize analyzes your system and makes the appropriate changes to your CONFIG.SYS and AUTOEXEC.BAT files.

QRAM uses its own versions of similar DOS device drivers (see Table 24.4).

You'll want to substitute the QRAM device drivers for the DOS device drivers in your system files.

Table 24.4. QRAM device drivers.

QRAM Version	*DOS Version*
QRAM.SYS	HIMEM.SYS/EMM386.EXE
LOADHI.SYS	`DEVICEHIGH`
LOADHI.COM	`LOADHIGH`

Like MOVE'EM, QRAM is a good way to manage your expanded memory if you have an older computer and an EMS memory card.

Wrapping It All Up

As you can see, most of these third-party memory management programs make it very easy to manage your memory—and, in some cases, go far beyond what is offered in DOS. Unless you have an older computer, however, I recommend sticking with DOS 6. Thanks to MEMMAKER, DOS 6 can do just about anything these third-party programs can do—and it's all built into the operating system!

25

Managing Windows Memory

Memory management under Microsoft Windows isn't that different from DOS—you just need more of it (memory, that is, not management). If you follow good memory management principles with DOS—and have lots of extended memory—you're 99 percent of the way to efficient Windows memory management.

All About How Windows Uses Memory

Windows is a memory hog. There, I said it. Windows need for memory is one of those truisms that civilized people seldom talk about in mixed company; it may be fear of Microsoft, or just denial of a lone liability in an otherwise first-rate operating environment. Whatever.

All the comments and advice given in this chapter apply specifically to Windows 3.1. If you're running Windows 3.0, most of this information applies verbatim, but some stuff will be slightly different. My advice is, if you're running Windows 3.0, it's time for you to upgrade to Windows 3.1. It actually runs a little smoother, uses memory a little better, and crashes less frequently. The combination of Windows 3.1 with DOS 6 is a match made in Microsoft heaven—the engineers in Washington state worked many long hours to ensure that these two programs work quite efficiently and effectively with each other.

What Windows Is and What It Does

You see, Windows isn't an operating *system* like DOS, it's an operating *environment* that sits on top of DOS. This means that you still use DOS to operate your system, and DOS still manages your system's memory—and uses the necessary resources for its own use.

Windows operates in addition to DOS. So you get a double memory hit—you have to load all the DOS BIOS and devices, as well as all sorts of Windows stuff. And Windows, because of its nifty graphical user interface (GUI) and ability to run more than one program at one time, can use a lot of memory.

Skip This, It's Technical!

GUIs use a lot of memory because it takes a large amount of data to display a screen composed entirely of graphics images. In fact, the higher the resolution you use to display Windows, the more memory is used. (SuperVGA takes more memory than VGA, in other words.) Most PCs come with video cards that include their own memory. These cards allow higher resolution displays and faster operation.

How Much Memory Does Windows Need?

As you can see, you just have to have more than normal conventional memory to run Windows. If your system only has 640K RAM, Windows simply won't run. (For that matter, you need an 80286 or better system to run Windows, as well.)

Windows makes good use of extended memory. It doesn't use expanded memory at all. The key factor here is that you need a system with lots of extended memory to run Windows. *Lots* is the operative word. Microsoft says you can run Windows on a system with 2M total memory. Reasonable people, however, take issue with that recommendation. I've found that 4M total memory is the minimum for acceptable performance, and more than that makes things run even better. (A system with 8M RAM runs pretty well, in my experience.)

PSST! The more programs you run, the more memory you need. If you only run one program at a time under Windows, you can get by with less memory. If you like to run multiple Windows applications on the same screen, it's time to stock up on DRAM chips!

Creating Memory on Your Hard Disk

Because Windows has such an insatiable hunger for memory, it sometimes needs more memory than you might have available on your system. For this reason, Windows can use free space on your hard disk to simulate normal random access memory. This kind of fake memory is called *virtual memory*, and it actually speeds up Windows operation quite a bit under certain high-load situations. Of course, it's better to just load up on the RAM, but it's a lot cheaper and easier to let Windows use 6M of your hard disk as virtual memory than it is to add an extra 6M RAM to your system.

Looking at Windows Memory

Because Windows counts both real RAM and virtual memory on your hard disk as available memory, you can't really get a true look at Windows use of RAM. You can, however, look at Windows RAM and disk memory as a whole.

To look at Windows memory, pull down the **H**elp menu in the Windows Program Manager and select the **A**bout Program Manager option. When the About Program Manager dialog box appears (as shown in Figure 25.1), you'll see some basic information about your version of Windows.

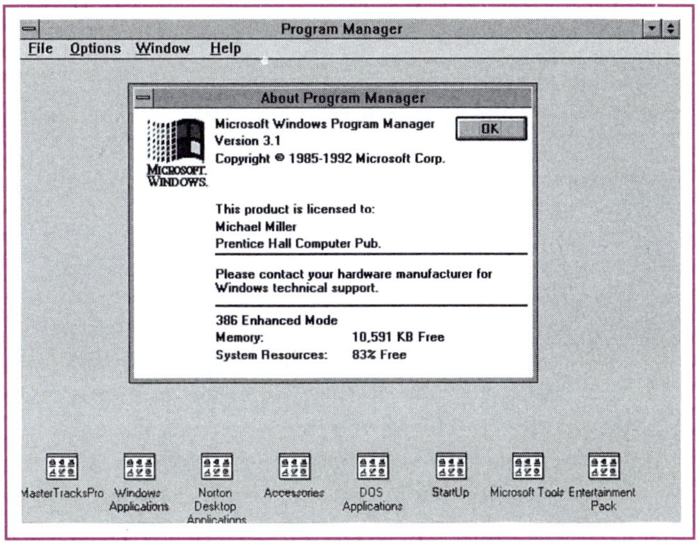

Figure 25.1. *The Windows About Program Manager dialog box, which displays memory and system resource use.*

Of primary importance is the memory measurement. Windows calculates how much memory is free (in K) on your system. Remember, though, that this includes both RAM and the disk space allocated to virtual memory. So, if you only have 4M RAM on your system and see that you have 6M memory free, don't think that your DRAM chips have somehow multiplied—Windows is simply counting the free disk space into the total memory figure!

Skip This, It's Technical!

Windows 3.1 has two separate operating modes, each generating different levels of performance and requiring different standards in hardware. The default (and preferred) operating mode is called *386 Enhanced Mode*. If, for some reason, your system can't run Windows in Enhanced Mode, you can force Windows to start in the lower-performance *Standard Mode* by typing `WIN /S` at the DOS prompt. If you can't use Enhanced Mode, consider adding more memory to your system or just plain buying a new computer—Enhanced Mode offers lots of advantages (including the ability to run DOS programs from within Windows) that you just don't get in Standard Mode.

This dialog box also displays the amount of *system resources* you have free. In Windows-speak, system resources include memory, disk space, and some other obscure stuff that you really don't want to know about. Suffice to say, the more free resources you have, the better. The lower the free resources, the more sluggish Windows becomes; if the number drops below 25 percent or so, prepare yourself for some frequent error messages and program glitches.

Yikes!

Here's something you probably didn't know: sometimes Windows has more resources than it thinks it has! You see, every time you run a program, it reserves a certain amount of resources—including memory—for its own use. When you close the program, it's supposed to release those resources so other programs can use them. However, some programs (including Ami Pro and Word for Windows) aren't that well behaved and don't release all the resources when they close. So, if you run Windows for an extended period of time, these unreleased memory chunks keep building up and taking away valuable resource space for whatever it is you're trying to do. The solution is simple—exit Windows from time to time. Whenever you close Windows, all the memory is released, so when you start Windows again, you start with a clean slate.

Of course, the better way to look at memory resources under Windows is to open a DOS window and execute the MEM command. It works as well under Windows as under plain DOS!

Setting Up DOS for Windows

If you plan on running Windows, there are a few things you need to keep in mind when you're setting up your CONFIG.SYS and AUTOEXEC.BAT files:

- Upgrade to DOS 6. It's better optimized for use with Windows than any previous version of DOS.
- When you run MEMMAKER, let it know that you're running Windows. Then run the Custom Setup and answer the questions on the Advanced options screen as follows:

  Specify which drivers and TSRs to include in optimization? (No.)

  Scan the upper memory area aggressively? (Yes.)

  Optimize upper memory for use with Windows? (Yes if you're using DOS programs as well as Windows programs; No if you're using Windows programs exclusively.)

  Use monochrome region (B000-BFFF) for running programs? (Yes if you have an EGA or VGA monitor; No if you have a SuperVGA or monochrome monitor.)

  Keep current EMS386 memory exclusions and inclusions? (No.)

  Move Extended BIOS Data Area from conventional to upper memory? (Yes.)

- Make sure you're using UMBs and the HMA efficiently; load DOS and any other drivers and programs high, if possible.
- Use SMARTDRV.EXE (in AUTOEXEC.BAT) instead of SMARTDRV.SYS (in CONFIG.SYS) to create a disk cache. If you have DOS 6, use the version of SMARTDRV.EXE installed in your DOS directory. Size the cache to equal about 25 percent of your available extended memory.

Yikes!

Whatever you do, don't load both SMARTDRV.SYS and SMARTDRV.EXE! This can freeze your system before you ever get going—open up your CONFIG.SYS file and delete any reference to SMARTDRV.SYS immediately!

- Don't create a RAM disk; you're better off just using a disk cache and leaving the rest of your extended memory free for Windows to use on its own.
- Don't even think about using expanded memory; if some of your programs need EMS, Windows simulates whatever is needed if you run the program from within Windows.

Of course, the most important thing to keep in mind is that you need as much extended memory as you can afford! Expanded memory won't do—get rid of your EMS card and go XMS exclusively. My recommendation is that you need 4M total memory, minimum, and things run a whole lot better if you have 8M or more.

Creating Virtual Memory

When you first install Windows, you're prompted to create virtual memory on your hard disk. Fortunately, you can also create (or change) virtual memory after installation.

Yikes!

You can only create virtual memory on 80386- or 80486-based computers.

To change your virtual memory setup, open the Windows Control Panel and double-click on the 386 Enhanced icon. When the 386 Enhanced dialog box appears, click on the Virtual Memory button to display the Virtual Memory dialog box. This dialog box displays your current virtual memory settings—the drive used, the size (in K), and the type (permanent or temporary).

To change these settings, click on the Change button; the Virtual Memory dialog box enlarges to include a New Settings area (as shown in Figure 25.2). From here you can change the drive used for virtual memory, the type of virtual memory (None, Temporary, or Permanent—Permanent is normally preferred), and the size of the virtual memory swap file. (Windows suggests a recommended size, which is normally a good recommendation.) When you do all the OK clicking, you'll have an area of your hard disk set aside for virtual memory use.

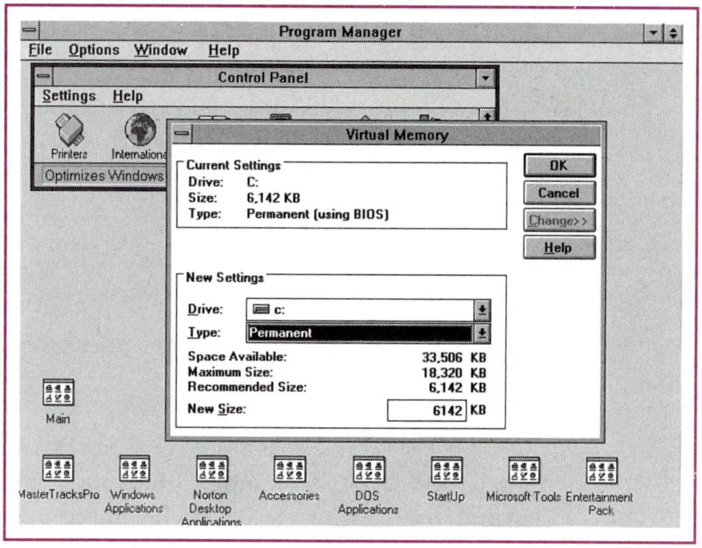

Figure 25.2. *The Virtual Memory dialog box expanded to include the New Settings area.*

Skip This, It's Technical!

Windows uses something called a *swap file* to create virtual memory. A swap file is a hidden file that Windows creates on your hard disk to swap information between your disk and your RAM. A *Permanent* swap file is created out of contiguous disk space, and a *Temporary* swap file is created on the fly out of whatever noncontiguous disk space is available. For this reason, a Permanent swap file is faster than a Temporary one. Also, you probably want to *defragment* your hard disk (see Appendix E, "Five Tips to Optimize Hard Disk Efficiency") before you create a virtual memory area—this frees up the contiguous disk space you need for a large swap file.

Should you use virtual memory? Sure, what's to lose? Naturally, it's preferable to run everything in RAM, but with Windows you often don't have all the RAM you need to do what you want to do. By all means, beef up your system's RAM, but still devote some disk space to virtual memory—you never know when it will come in handy!

Running DOS Programs in Windows

Running Windows programs in Windows is one thing. Trying to run DOS programs from within Windows is a whole 'nother situation. Let's take a peek at what you need to do to run DOS stuff from Windows without causing everything to come crashing down about your ears!

Making Sure DOS Memory Is Maximized

When you run a DOS program from within Windows, it's kind of like running a little version of DOS itself from within a DOS window.

With that in mind, it really pays to practice good DOS memory management techniques. In particular, you need to free up as much conventional memory as possible to run your DOS applications. When you're setting up your system's memory, be sure you're using UMBs and the HMA to load as many programs and device drivers as possible—thus moving them out of conventional memory and leaving more space for DOS programs.

Creating PIF Files

To maximize the way your DOS programs use memory from within Windows, you need to create a *program information file* (PIF) for each DOS program. A PIF file (okay, I know the term *PIF file* is redundant, but that's what everyone calls 'em!) lets you configure various options about how Windows runs your DOS program.

To create (or edit) a PIF file, you have to use the PIF Editor, which is located in the Main program group in the Windows Program Manager. When you double-click on the PIF Editor icon, the PIF Editor's main window appears (see Figure 25.3). From here you can pull down the **File** menu to **O**pen an existing PIF file or simply create a new file (and **S**ave it under a new filename).

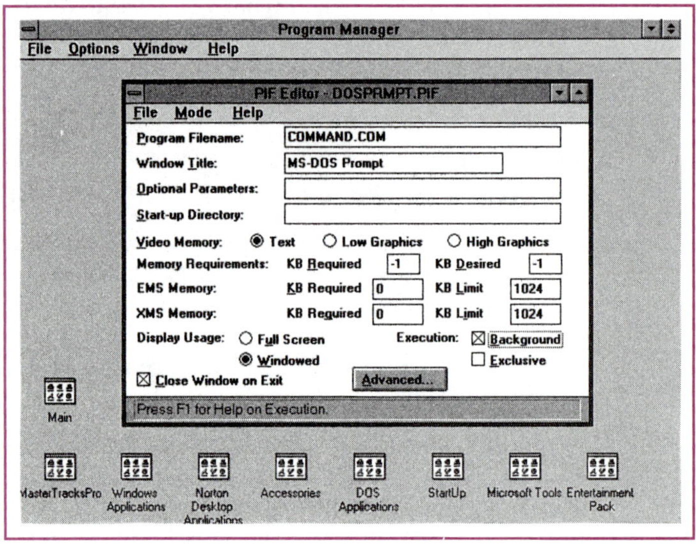

Figure 25.3. *The main PIF Editor window.*

As you can see, there's lots of stuff required to create a PIF file. Let's look at the basic options in Table 25.1.

Table 25.1. PIF options.

Program Filename	This is the program's .EXE filename, with complete directory path information.
Window Title	This is what you call the program, as it appears in the title bar of the window.
Optional Parameters	These are any command-line options needed to properly start the program.
Start-up Directory	If your program needs to start from a certain directory, note it here.
Video Memory	If your application runs in anything other than straight text mode (i.e., if it uses any graphics screens), note it here. The higher the graphics mode selected, the more memory Windows sets aside for graphics use of this application.
Memory Requirements	This selection lets you determine how Windows assigns conventional memory to your DOS application. The KB Required sets the minimum amount of memory assigned to the application; the KB Desired sets the maximum amount of memory available to the application. (Advice: set both KB Required and KB Desired to -1, which sends all available RAM to the program.)

continues

Table 25.1. continued

EMS Memory	Use this setting if your application uses expanded memory. Normally the KB Required should be set to 0 and the KB Limit set to whatever is needed by the program; 0 is fine here, too.
XMS Memory	Use this setting if your application uses extended memory. Set KB Required to 0 and the KB Limit to a minimum of 1,024.
Display Usage	If your application can run in a window, set it as such. If it needs to be seen full-screen (for example, if it uses a lot of graphics), then set it that way.
Execution	Unless your program needs all your system's resources, set it to run in the background; this way you can run other programs while the DOS program is doing its thing.
Close Window on Exit	Just check this one—otherwise you're left with a window showing the DOS prompt when you close the program!

There are even more memory options available if you click on the Advanced button. The Advanced Options dialog box, shown in Figure 25.4, includes lots of obscure options that you don't really need to configure but can if you want to.

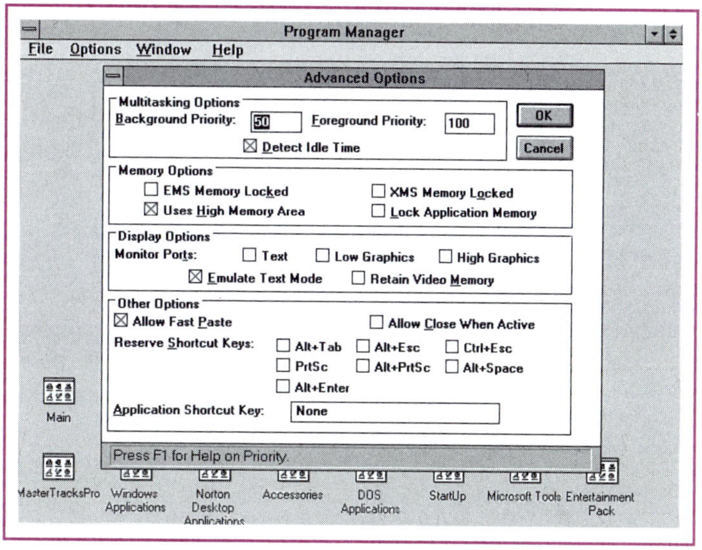

Figure 25.4. *The Advanced Options dialog box.*

I won't go into all the options here because they don't directly apply to memory usage, but I will mention the Memory Options section. The options here include those shown in Table 25.2.

Table 25.2. Advanced memory options.

EMS Memory Locked	When checked, this option prevents any expanded memory used by this application to be swapped to the hard disk as virtual memory. Because this can slow down your complete system (while speeding up the particular application), I recommend that you don't check this box.

continues

Table 25.2. continued

Uses High Memory Area	When checked, this option allows the application to use the HMA, if available. I recommend that you do check this box.
XMS Memory Locked	When checked, this option prevents any extended memory used by this application to be swapped to the hard disk as virtual memory. Because this can slow down your complete system (while speeding up the particular application), I recommend that you don't check this box.
Lock Application Memory	When checked, this option prevents the application from releasing any conventional memory used when data is swapped to the hard disk as virtual memory. Although this might make your specific application run slightly faster, it can cause other applications not to have enough RAM to run. I recommend that you don't check this box.

After you create a PIF file for a DOS application, be sure you launch the PIF file rather than the normal program file! That's right, if you make a PIF file for 1-2-3, execute the 123.PIF file instead of the normal 123.EXE file—or else all your careful memory management may be for naught!

Wrapping It All Up

Actually, if you're managing your DOS memory well, you don't have to do much more if you're running Windows. Just be sure you have lots of extended memory, free up as much conventional and extended memory as possible, and use PIF files to start any DOS programs from within Windows. Sounds simple, doesn't it?

26

Adding Memory to Your System

You know, it's no fun managing memory if you don't have enough memory to manage. So let's take a look at just how you can beef up the memory on your system without a lot of fuss and bother.

First, You Buy Some Chips

Before you shop for your chips, you need to determine what kind of chips to buy. Normally this is dictated by your computer system. Consult your PC's instruction manual to see what kind of additional memory your manufacturer recommends.

Most PCs use DRAM (dynamic random access memory) chips for memory. You can buy DRAM chips in different configurations—the configuration you choose should match the sockets on your motherboard. You can choose from DIPs, SIMMs, SIPs, and ZIPs (all explained way back in Chapter 3, "Where Is My System's Memory?"), although more often than not your system will use DIPs (dual in-line package) or SIMMs (single in-line memory module). It's possible that you can't (or you just don't want to) add chips directly to your motherboard, and therefore you have to use a memory expansion card instead. If this is the case, you need to fill up the card with chips before you insert it into your system unit.

Of course, if you're adding expanded memory (EMS) to your system, you don't add individual chips; you add an *expanded memory card*. Most cards come with an EMS driver to manage your system's use of the expanded memory—or you can use a third-party memory manager (like MOVE'EM or QRAM) to manage your EMS memory.

When shopping for your chips, be sure you get the fastest chips your system can use—and that you can afford! Look at the chip's access time (lower is better), wait state (lower is better), and capability to interleave (which is good). Remember, the faster the chip, the faster your system can access memory.

Finally, you need to determine what size DRAM chip to buy. The size is determined by what your system requires, and DRAM chips are measured in bits (not bytes). DIP chips come in 64K, 256K, and 1M sizes; SIMMs typically come in one-megabyte banks of nine chips.

Next, You Install the Chips

It's deceptively easy to add memory to your computer. Whether you're installing a memory expansion card or plugging some chips into their sockets, it's just not that tough—if you know what you're doing!

You can install memory either on a memory expansion card or directly on your motherboard. If you have a choice, choose the motherboard. Memory on the motherboard often works faster than the same RAM chips installed on a memory expansion card, because the bus on the motherboard is normally faster than the bus to the expansion slot (things work faster if they're hooked up directly). In essence, it pays to bypass the middleman—in this case, the expansion card/slot combination.

Skip This, It's Technical!

Not only can you add memory to your system, you can also replace your existing memory with chips that give you more memory. For example, if you're using 256K chips, you can upgrade to 1M chips and quadruple your available memory! The only thing you have to note is that you can't just replace a single chip—if you upgrade one, you have to upgrade all of them!

Installing a Memory Expansion Card

Installing a memory expansion card is very simple—whether it's an EMS expanded memory card or a normal memory expansion card full of DRAM chips for extended memory use.

First, if you have a normal expansion card, you have to put some chips on it. That's right, most memory expansion cards come rather empty. You need to buy the right kind of chips (as recommended by the card's manufacturer) and plug 'em in the sockets before you even think about taking the top off your computer.

Next, take the top off your computer. (Be sure your system unit is turned off and unplugged, of course.) Now identify an open *expansion slot*, normally located in the rear of the system unit. (You'll find other cards filling up some of the slots already.) Slide the card down into the socket, making sure it is seated securely. Now you can button up the box, plug it in, and turn it on.

Skip This, It's Technical!

If you install an EMS expanded memory card and have less than 640K memory on your system, you have to use the EMS expanded memory manager to *backfill* conventional memory with expanded memory. (Backfilling allows you to increase the memory on a PC with less than 640K memory to the full 640K level using expanded memory.) You may also need to reset some switches on your computer's motherboard to disable some of your conventional memory.

Installing DIP Chips

Installing chips isn't as hard as it might seem. You need to take certain precautions and take extreme care, but it really comes down to a matter of plugging chips into sockets.

Begin by turning off and unplugging your system unit. Next, take the top off the box. Now you get to look for your RAM chip sockets. As explained in Chapter 3, there is no one place where all PC manufacturers place their RAM chip sockets; all you know is that they're somewhere on your motherboard (the big circuit board at the bottom of your system unit that just about everything else plugs into).

Most PCs have *banks* of sockets for RAM chips. This is because you never insert just one chip; you always insert a bank of chips to get to the memory level you desire. Banks normally hold either 9, 18, or 36 chips each. If you can't find your RAM banks, check the instruction manual of your PC; it should include a schematic of the motherboard.

Yikes!

Don't shock your chips! Because static electricity can completely fry RAM chips, be sure you discharge any static electricity from your body before embarking on the chip installation routine. (Just touch something metal; it grounds you and eliminates any built-up charges.)

If you're installing a DIP chip (which has nothing at all to do with chip dip), you have to line the chip up with the socket. (Normally there's a dot or notch on the socket to guide the way.) Then (very carefully) align every leg on the chip with the corresponding holes in the socket. Once each leg is in place, give the chip a gentle push, and—if you did everything right—the chip should be firmly inserted in its socket.

When all your chips are inserted, you can button up your system unit, plug it in, and turn it on. In other words, you're back in business!

Yikes!

Actually, you may want to check out your system before you box it back up. This way you can easily locate and fix any problems without having to open the darned thing up again!

Installing SIMM Chips

The second most common type of DRAM chip is the SIMM chip. A SIMM chip is actually a very small board that holds several individual chips. In most computers, a RAM bank holds four SIMMs, and you have to fill each bank full.

Installing a SIMM chip is actually a little easier than installing a DIP chip. As before, turn off and unplug your system unit, then take the cover off. Once you locate the SIMM chip banks, you have to line the metal edge connector with the slot on the socket, as shown in Figure 26.1. Then insert the SIMM at an angle into the slot. When the edge of the SIMM is in the slot, rotate the SIMM until it clicks into place.

Figure 26.1.
Inserting a SIMM chip.

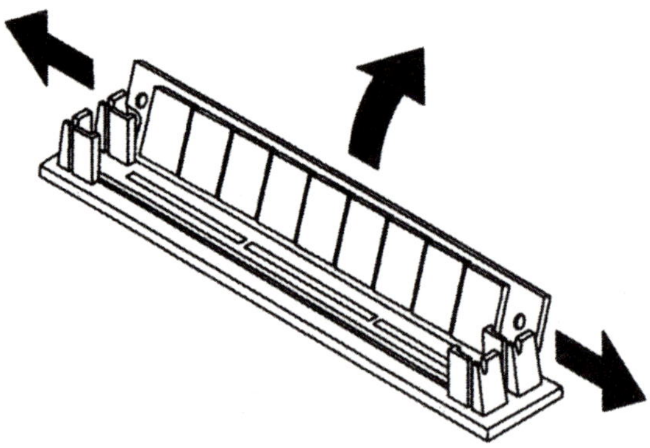

When your SIMMs are all in place, you can button up your system unit and get back to work!

Finally, Reconfigure Your System

Just because you've inserted your card or chips onto the motherboard, figured out how to get the case back on the system unit, and screwed all the screws back in, doesn't mean you're done. Now you need to tell your system all about that new memory you just added.

When your computer boots up, you need to run your PC's setup program. (How you do this differs from system to system, so consult your user's manual for instructions.) Your setup program configures your system's CMOS memory (a nonvolatile ROM chip that contains essential system setup information) to recognize the additional memory you just added. When this is done, reboot your system again, and you should be set.

PSST! 

Most software programs (including Windows) automatically pick up on the fact that more memory is available. Some applications, however—older ones in particular—may need to be reconfigured to recognize the added memory.

Wrapping It All Up

Well, that just about does it for Section II of this book. If you've taken a cue from our friend the elephant and plodded through all this information, you now know exactly how to add memory to your system, as well as how to configure your system to use all the memory you installed. What you don't know yet, however, is which configuration to use for your particular system. Well, my friend, help is on the way! Just move ahead to Section III, "Easy Memory Setups Anyone Can Do," where you'll find easy memory setups for just about any system you can think of!

Part III

Easy Memory Setups Anyone Can Do

This section of the book includes just a ton of recommended memory setups, all keyed to specific system configurations. Just look at the chapter line up:

But how do you determine which memory setup you should use? What if you're running both DOS 6 and Windows? What do you do then, huh?

Hey! Don't get all wound up, okay? I'll make it easy for you, if you just pay attention. So turn the page to Chapter 27, "Determining the Best Memory Setups to Use."

27

Determining the Best Memory Setups to Use

Before you can set up your setup, you need to know what kind of setup to set up, so follow the instructions in this chapter and you'll be able to figure out which setup to set up. Is that clear?

First Things First—How Is Your System Configured?

The first determining factor is which operating system you're using. Run through the following checklist and see what it tells you:

Question #1: ***Are you using DOS, OS/2, or UNIX as your operating system?*** If you're running OS/2 or UNIX, you've got the wrong book. (How did you get this far?) If you're running DOS, proceed to Question #2.

Question #2: ***Are you running MS-DOS, PC DOS, or DR DOS?*** If you're running DR DOS, you've got the wrong book. (Sorry!) If you're running MS-DOS or PC DOS, proceed to Question #3.

Question #3 ***Are you running Windows?*** If you're running Windows, you need Chapter 30, "The Best Memory Setups If You're Running an Older Version of DOS." If you're not running Windows, proceed to Question #4.

Question #4: ***Are you using DOS 4 (or an earlier version), DOS 5, or DOS 6?*** If you're running DOS 4 or an earlier version, you need Chapter 30, "The Best Memory Setups If You're Running an Older Version of DOS." If you're running DOS 5, you need Chapter 29, "The Best Memory Setups If You're Running DOS 5." If you're running DOS 6, you need Chapter 28, "The Best Memory Setups If You're Running DOS 6."

Got all that?

In spite of the preceding checklist, you may want to read two chapters if you're using Windows. That is, if you're using Windows with DOS 6, you might find it useful (but not absolutely necessary) to read both Chapter 28 and Chapter 31.

Taking It All with a Grain of Salt

Now, the memory setups recommended in the following chapters are just that—recommendations. It's possible that you can come up with better configurations on your own; if so, good for you!

It really is true that, like snowflakes, no two computer systems are identical. There may be something about the specific programs you use or your specific hardware setup that requires a slight spin on my recommended memory setup. So while my recommendations may not squeeze every last byte of memory from your particular system, I do guarantee that they will do a darned good job and be more than good enough for most users. Okay?

Wrapping It All Up

It's time. Can't you feel it? After 27 chapters of build-up and suspense, you finally get to discover the perfect memory setup for your computer system. Well, don't let me delay you any longer—turn the page and let's get down to business!

28

The Best Memory Setups If You're Running DOS 6

This chapter cuts right to the chase and tells you the best memory setups if you're running DOS 6. You won't learn how to make all these changes to your system, however; you need to refer to Section II, "Managing Your System's Memory," for information on how to edit your system files, add memory, use MEMMAKER, and perform other essential memory management operations.

The setups listed in this chapter are the setups I recommend for your particular system. There are other setups you can use—these are the ones I prefer in today's computing environment. I generally prefer extended memory (when available) over expanded memory because Windows and most newer DOS programs use XMS, not EMS.

To figure out which setup to use, you first have to know what kind of microprocessor you have on your system. Then you have the choice of DOS-only or Windows setups. Choose the right setup for your particular system configuration, and before you know it, you'll have more free memory than you'll know what to do with!

Using MEMMAKER to Set Up Your System

The best way to set up your computer with DOS 6 is to use MEMMAKER. MEMMAKER makes essential changes to your CONFIG.SYS and AUTOEXEC.BAT files to maximize your system's use of memory. After you run MEMMAKER, you can go back and edit your system files to make any minor changes necessary to tweak the last byte of RAM out of your system. To run MEMMAKER, type the following line at the DOS prompt:

```
MEMMAKER
```

See Chapter 23, "Working with DOS 6 Memory Management Tools," for more details on using MEMMAKER to optimize your memory use with DOS 6.

Running DOS 6 on an 8088/8086-Based System

DOS 6 doesn't give you a lot of options with a system based on either the 8088 or 8086 microprocessors. In fact, if you want to utilize more than the conventional 640K memory, you need to install an EMS memory expansion board and configure your system to run expanded memory.

The Basic Setup

Consider these options for a basic 8088/8086-based system:

- Install an expanded memory card in your system unit. Be sure the card conforms to the LIM standard and is filled with as much memory as possible (try for at least 2M).
- Install the expanded memory manager that came with your EMS card to your hard disk, then add a line to your CONFIG.SYS file to load the EMS driver into memory.
- Install a third-party memory manager designed specifically for 8088/8086-based PCs, such as MOVE'EM or QRAM. You'll need to add a line to your CONFIG.SYS file to load the memory manager into memory.
- Create a disk cache, using the driver supplied with your third-party memory manager. The cache should take up approximately 25 percent of your available expanded memory.
- Create a RAM disk using the driver supplied with your third-party memory manager. The RAM disk should take up approximately 25 percent of your available expanded memory.
- Be sure you correctly set up your software programs to utilize your new expanded memory.

Of course, the better option may be to buy a new PC—you would be amazed at how much faster a new 80486 is than your old 8088/8086!

Running Windows

Are you kidding me? You can't run Windows on an 8088/8086-based system! Give it up and buy a newer computer, for gosh sakes!

Running DOS 6 on an 80286-Based System

You have quite a few more options available to you if you're running an 80286-based system. I recommend you add extended memory to your system, especially if you're using newer DOS-based programs or Windows; it's a more popular way to go than the older expanded memory.

The Basic Setup

Consider these options for a basic 80286-based system:

- Add as much extended memory to your system as possible; try to get your system to at least 4M total memory.
- Add the following lines to your CONFIG.SYS file in the following order; if they (or some variation) are not there, add them:

```
DEVICE=HIMEM.SYS
DOS=HIGH
```

- Load any other device drivers in your CONFIG.SYS file with the `DEVICE` command.

- Load any device drivers in your AUTOEXEC.BAT file normally with a simple command line.
- Create a disk cache by adding the following line to your AUTOEXEC.BAT file (`xxxx` should equal about 25 percent of your available extended memory, in K):

  ```
  SMARTDRV.EXE XXXX
  ```

- Create a RAM drive by adding the following line to your CONFIG.SYS file (`xxxx` should equal about 25 percent of your available extended memory, in K):

  ```
  DEVICE=RAMDRIVE.SYS XXXX /E
  ```

- Change the `BUFFERS`, `FILES`, `FCBS` (if present), and `STACKS` statements in your CONFIG.SYS file to read:

  ```
  BUFFERS=10,0
  FILES=20
  FCBS=1
  STACKS=0,0
  ```

If you prefer to use expanded memory (or have older DOS-based programs that use expanded memory), see the options presented for 8088/8086-based PCs.

Running Windows

The setup, if you're running Windows, is similar to that if you're running only DOS-based programs; the difference is that you don't need to create a RAM disk (you want to free as much extended memory as possible for Windows use).

Consider the following options for an 80286-based system running Windows:

- Add as much extended memory to your system as possible; try to get your system to at least 4M total memory.

- Add the following lines to your CONFIG.SYS file in the following order; if they (or some variation) are not there, add them:

```
DEVICE=HIMEM.SYS
DOS=HIGH
```

- Load any other device drivers in your CONFIG.SYS file with the `DEVICE` command.
- Load any device drivers in your AUTOEXEC.BAT file normally with a simple command line.
- Create a disk cache by adding the following line to your AUTOEXEC.BAT file:

```
SMARTDRV.EXE
```

- Change the `BUFFERS`, `FILES`, `FCBS` (if present), and `STACKS` statements in your CONFIG.SYS file to read:

```
BUFFERS=10,0
FILES=20
FCBS=1
STACKS=0,0
```

Running DOS 6 on an 80386- or 80486-Based System

If you have an 80386 or better system, you can use the EMM386.EXE memory manager to create upper memory blocks, which give you more options when maximizing your memory usage. Again, if you have the choice, I recommend using extended memory on your system; it's simply the way most newer DOS and Windows programs work.

The Basic Setup

Consider these options for a basic 80386/80486-based system:

- Add as much extended memory to your system as possible; try to get your system to at least 4M total memory.
- Run MEMMAKER (using the Express Setup) to optimize your system.
- Be sure the following lines are present in your CONFIG.SYS file in the following order; if they (or some variation) are not there, add them:

```
DEVICE=HIMEM.SYS
DEVICE=EMM386.EXE NOEMS
DOS=HIGH, UMB
```

- Load any other device drivers in your CONFIG.SYS file with the `DEVICEHIGH` command.
- Load any device drivers in your AUTOEXEC.BAT file with the `LOADHIGH` (or `LH`) command.
- Create a disk cache by adding the following line to your AUTOEXEC.BAT file (`XXXX` should equal about 25 percent of your available extended memory, in K):

```
LOADHIGH=SMARTDRV.EXE XXXX
```

- Create a RAM drive by adding the following line to your CONFIG.SYS file (`XXXX` should equal about 25 percent of your available extended memory, in K):

```
DEVICEHIGH=RAMDRIVE.SYS XXXX /E
```

- Change the `BUFFERS`, `FILES`, `FCBS` (if present), and `STACKS` statements in your CONFIG.SYS file to read:

```
BUFFERS=10,0
FILES=20
FCBS=1
STACKS=0,0
```

If you prefer to use expanded memory (or have older DOS-based programs that use expanded memory), see the options presented for an 8088/8086-based system.

Running Windows

The setup, if you're running Windows, is similar to the one used if you're running only DOS-based programs; the difference is that you don't need to create a RAM disk (you want to free as much extended memory as possible for Windows use).

Consider these options for an 80386/80486-based system running Windows:

- Add as much extended memory to your system as possible; try to get your system to at least 4M total memory.
- Run MEMMAKER using the Custom Setup. Answer the questions on the Advanced options screen as follows:

  Specify which drivers and TSRs to include in optimization? (No.)

  Scan the upper memory area aggressively? (Yes.)

  Optimize upper memory for use with Windows? (Yes, if you're using DOS programs as well as Windows programs; No, if you're using Windows programs exclusively.)

  Use monochrome region (B000-BFFF) for running programs? (Yes, if you have an EGA or VGA monitor; No, if you have a SuperVGA or monochrome monitor.)

  Keep current EMS386 memory exclusions and inclusions? (No.)

  Move Extended BIOS Data Area from conventional to upper memory? (Yes.)

- Be sure the following lines are present in your CONFIG.SYS file in the following order; if they (or some variation) are not there, add them:

```
DEVICE=HIMEM.SYS
DEVICE=EMM386.EXE NOEMS
DOS=HIGH, UMB
```

- Load any other device drivers in your CONFIG.SYS file with the `DEVICEHIGH` command.
- Load any device drivers in your AUTOEXEC.BAT file with the `LOADHIGH` (or `LH`) command.
- Create a disk cache by adding the following line to your AUTOEXEC.BAT file (`XXXX` should equal about 25 percent of your available extended memory, in K):

```
LOADHIGH=SMARTDRV.EXE
```

- Change the `BUFFERS`, `FILES`, `FCBS` (if present), and `STACKS` statements in your CONFIG.SYS file to read:

```
BUFFERS=10,0
FILES=20
FCBS=1
STACKS=0,0
```

- Create virtual memory on your hard disk by opening the Windows Control Panel and double-clicking on the 386 Enhanced icon. When the 386 Enhanced dialog box appears, click on the Virtual Memory button to display the Virtual Memory dialog box. Click on the Change button and enter new settings for the amount of disk space you want to devote to virtual memory.

Wrapping It All Up

If you have DOS 6, your setup is easy. In fact, if you do nothing more than run MEMMAKER in Express Setup, you'll be 95 percent of the way there. Congratulations—you're now an efficient memory manager!

29

The Best Memory Setups If You're Running DOS 5

This chapter gets right down to business and describes the best memory setups if you're running DOS 5. You won't learn how to make all these changes to your system, however; you need to refer to Section II, "Managing Your System's Memory," for information on how to edit your system files, add memory, and perform other essential memory management operations.

HMM...

The setups listed in this chapter are the setups I recommend for your particular system. There are other setups you can use—these are the ones I prefer in today's computing environment. I generally prefer extended memory (when available) over expanded memory because Windows and most newer DOS programs use XMS, not EMS.

To figure out which setup to use, you first have to know what kind of microprocessor you have on your system. Then you have the choice of DOS-only or Windows setups. Choose the right setup for your particular system configuration, and before you know it, you'll have more free memory than you'll know what to do with!

Running DOS 5 on an 8088/8086-Based System

DOS 5, like DOS 6, doesn't give you a lot of options with a system based on either the 8088 or 8086 microprocessors. In fact, if you want to utilize more than the conventional 640K memory, you need to install an EMS memory expansion board and configure your system to run expanded memory.

The Basic Setup

Consider these options for a basic 8088/8086-based system:

- Install an expanded memory card in your system unit. Be sure the card conforms to the LIM standard, and is filled with as much memory as possible (try for at least 2M).
- Install the expanded memory manager that came with your EMS card to your hard disk, then add a line to your CONFIG.SYS file to load the EMS driver into memory.

- Install a third-party memory manager designed specifically for 8088/8086-based PCs, such as MOVE'EM or QRAM. You need to add a line to your CONFIG.SYS file to load the memory manager into memory.
- Create a disk cache using the driver supplied with your third-party memory manager. The cache should take up approximately 25 percent of your available expanded memory.
- Create a RAM disk using the driver supplied with your third-party memory manager. The RAM disk should take up approximately 25 percent of your available expanded memory.
- Be sure you correctly set up your software programs to utilize your new expanded memory.

Of course, the better option may be to buy a new PC—you would be amazed at how much faster a new 80486 is than your old 8088/8086!

Running Windows

Come on, you know better than to try to run Windows on an 8088/8086-based system! If you want to run Windows, you need a new PC.

Running DOS 5 on an 80286-Based System

You have quite a few more options available to you if you're running an 80286-based system. I recommend adding extended memory to your system, especially if you're using newer DOS-based programs or Windows (it's a more popular way to go than the older expanded memory).

The Basic Setup

Consider these options for a basic 80286-based system:

- Add as much extended memory to your system as possible; try to get your system to at least 4M total memory.
- Add the following lines to your CONFIG.SYS file in the following order:

```
DEVICE=HIMEM.SYS
DOS=HIGH
```

- Load any other device drivers in your CONFIG.SYS file with the `DEVICE` command.
- Load any device drivers in your AUTOEXEC.BAT file normally with a simple command line.
- Create a disk cache by adding the following line to your CONFIG.SYS file (`XXXX` should equal about 25 percent of your available extended memory, in K):

```
DEVICE=SMARTDRV.SYS XXXX
```

- Create a RAM drive by adding the following line to your CONFIG.SYS file (`XXXX` should equal about 25 percent of your available extended memory, in K):

```
DEVICE=RAMDRIVE.SYS XXXX /E
```

- Change the `BUFFERS`, `FILES`, `FCBS` (if present), and `STACKS` statements in your CONFIG.SYS file to read:

```
BUFFERS=10,0
FILES=20
FCBS=1,0
STACKS=0,0
```

If you prefer to use expanded memory (or have older DOS-based programs that use expanded memory), see the options presented for 8088/8086-based PCs.

Running Windows

The setup if you're running Windows is similar to the one used if you're running only DOS-based programs. The difference is that you don't need to create a RAM disk—use SMARTDRV.EXE instead of SMARTDRV.SYS (you need to specify an additional parameter for your disk cache).

Consider these options for an 80286-based system running Windows:

- Add as much extended memory to your system as possible; try to get your system to at least 4M total memory.
- Add the following lines to your CONFIG.SYS file in the following order:

  ```
  DEVICE=HIMEM.SYS
  DOS=HIGH
  ```

- Load any other device drivers in your CONFIG.SYS file with the `DEVICE` command.
- Load any device drivers in your AUTOEXEC.BAT file normally with a simple command line.
- Create a disk cache by adding the following line to your AUTOEXEC.BAT file (`xxxx` should equal about 25 percent of your available extended memory, in K):

  ```
  SMARTDRV.EXE XXXX 0
  ```

- Change the `BUFFERS`, `FILES`, `FCBS` (if present), and `STACKS` statements in your CONFIG.SYS file to read:

  ```
  BUFFERS=10,0
  FILES=20
  FCBS=1,0
  STACKS=0,0
  ```

Running DOS 5 on an 80386- or 80486-Based System

If you have an 80386 or better system, you can use the EMM386.EXE memory manager to create upper memory blocks, which give you more options when maximizing your memory usage. Again, if you have the choice, I recommend using extended memory on your system; it's simply the way most newer DOS and Windows programs work.

The Basic Setup

Consider these options for a basic 80386/80486-based system:

- Add as much extended memory to your system as possible; try to get your system to at least 4M total memory.
- Add the following lines to your CONFIG.SYS file in the following order:

```
DEVICE=HIMEM.SYS
DEVICE=EMM386.EXE NOEMS
DOS=HIGH, UMB
```

- Load any other device drivers in your CONFIG.SYS file with the `DEVICEHIGH` command.
- Load any device drivers in your AUTOEXEC.BAT file with the `LOADHIGH` (or `LH`) command.
- Create a disk cache by adding the following line to your CONFIG.SYS file (`XXXX` should equal about 25 percent of your available extended memory, in K):

```
DEVICEHIGH=SMARTDRV.SYS XXXX
```

- Create a RAM drive by adding the following line to your CONFIG.SYS file (`XXXX` should equal about 25 percent of your available extended memory, in K):

```
DEVICEHIGH=RAMDRIVE.SYS XXXX /E
```

- Change the `BUFFERS`, `FILES`, `FCBS` (if present), and `STACKS` statements in your CONFIG.SYS file to read:

```
BUFFERS=10,0
FILES=20
FCBS=1,0
STACKS=0,0
```

If you prefer to use expanded memory (or have older DOS-based programs that use expanded memory), see the options presented for an 8088/8086-based system.

Running Windows

The setup, if you're running Windows, is similar to the one used if you're running only DOS-based programs; the difference is that you don't need to create a RAM disk, you use SMARTDRV.EXE instead of SMARTDRV.SYS, and you need to specify an additional parameter for your disk cache.

Consider these options for an 80386/80486-based system running Windows:

- Add as much extended memory to your system as possible; try to get your system to at least 4M total memory.

- Add the following lines to your CONFIG.SYS file in the following order:

```
DEVICE=HIMEM.SYS
DEVICE=EMM386.EXE NOEMS
DOS=HIGH, UMB
```

- Load any other device drivers in your CONFIG.SYS file with the `DEVICEHIGH` command.
- Load any device drivers in your AUTOEXEC.BAT file with the `LOADHIGH` (or `LH`) command.
- Create a disk cache by adding the following line to your AUTOEXEC.BAT file (`XXXX` should equal about 25 percent of your available extended memory, in K):

```
LOADHIGH=SMARTDRV.EXE XXXX 0
```

- Change the `BUFFERS`, `FILES`, `FCBS` (if present), and `STACKS` statements in your CONFIG.SYS file to read:

```
BUFFERS=10,0
FILES=20
FCBS=1,0
STACKS=0,0
```

- Create virtual memory on your hard disk by opening the Windows Control Panel and double-clicking on the 386 Enhanced icon. When the 386 Enhanced dialog box appears, click on the Virtual Memory button to display the Virtual Memory dialog box. Click on the Change button and enter new settings for the amount of disk space you want to devote to virtual memory.

Wrapping It All Up

As you can see, your memory setup with DOS 5 is similar—but not identical—to the DOS 6 setup. Because you don't have MEMMAKER to do most of the work for you, be careful when implementing these changes! (Or, you can just upgrade to DOS 6, which might be easier when it's all said and done.)

30

The Best Memory Setups If You're Running an Older Version of DOS

This chapter gets right down to business and describes the best memory setups if you're running any version of DOS prior to DOS 5. You won't learn how to make all these changes to your system, however; you need to refer to Section II, "Managing Your System's Memory," for information on how to edit your system files, add memory, and perform other essential memory management operations.

The setups listed in this chapter are the setups I recommend for your particular system. There are other setups you can use, although these are the ones I prefer in today's computing environment. I generally prefer extended memory (when available) over expanded memory, because Windows and most newer DOS programs use XMS, not EMS.

To figure out which setup to use, you first have to know what kind of microprocessor you have on your system. Then you have the choice of DOS-only or Windows setups. Choose the right setup for your particular system configuration—and before you know it, you'll have more free memory than you know what to do with!

PSST!

Before you read about the pre-DOS 5 memory setups, listen to this one little bit of advice from someone who should know: *upgrade your system to DOS 6!* This is an easier way to fix your management problems than anything I can recommend in this chapter.

Running DOS 4 or Before on an 8088/8086-Based System

No version of DOS—including the older versions—gives you a lot of options with a system based on either the 8088 or 8086 microprocessors. In fact, if you want to utilize more than the conventional 640K memory, you need to install an EMS memory expansion board and configure your system to run expanded memory.

The Basic Setup

Consider these options for a basic 8088/8086-based system:

- Install an expanded memory card in your system unit. Be sure the card conforms to the LIM standard and is filled with as much memory as possible (try for at least 2M).
- Install the expanded memory manager that came with your EMS card to your hard disk, then add a line to your CONFIG.SYS file to load the EMS driver into memory.
- Install a third-party memory manager designed specifically for 8088/8086-based PCs, such as MOVE'EM or QRAM. You need to add a line to your CONFIG.SYS file to load the memory manager into memory.
- Create a disk cache using the driver supplied with your third-party memory manager. The cache should take up approximately 25 percent of your available expanded memory.
- Create a RAM disk using the driver supplied with your third-party memory manager. The RAM disk should take up approximately 25 percent of your available expanded memory.
- Be sure you correctly set up your software programs to utilize your new expanded memory.

Of course, the better option may be to buy a new PC—being sure it comes with DOS 6 preinstalled!

Running Windows

Haven't you learned by now? You can't run Windows on these older PCs! Save your bucks and buy a new system if you want to go GUI!

Running DOS 4 or Before on an 80286-Based System

Unfortunately, older versions of DOS don't give you many options you can use on an 80286-based system, either. You really need to add a third-party memory manager to use any extended memory at all. (I recommend extended over expanded memory—it's still the best way to go, even with these older versions of DOS.)

The Basic Setup

Consider these options for a basic 80286-based system:

- Add as much extended memory to your system as possible; try to get your system to at least 4M total memory.
- Install a third-party memory manager designed specifically for 80286-based PCs, such as MOVE'EM or QRAM. You need to add a line to your CONFIG.SYS file to load the memory manager into memory.
- Create a disk cache using the driver supplied with your third-party memory manager. The cache should take up approximately 25 percent of your available expanded memory.

- Create a RAM disk using the driver supplied with your third-party memory manager. The RAM disk should take up approximately 25 percent of your available expanded memory.

If you prefer to use expanded memory (or have older DOS-based programs that use expanded memory), see the options presented for 8088/8086-based PCs.

Running Windows

Your memory setup with Windows is quite different from your memory setup under DOS because Windows includes HIMEM.SYS and SMARTDRV.EXE files (not included with DOS 4). These tools can be used in place of a third-party memory management solution.

Consider these options for an 80286-based system running Windows:

- Add as much extended memory to your system as possible; try to get your system to at least 4M total memory.
- Add the following line to your CONFIG.SYS file:

  ```
  DEVICE=HIMEM.SYS
  ```

- Load any other device drivers in your CONFIG.SYS file with the `DEVICE` command.
- Load any device drivers in your AUTOEXEC.BAT file normally with a simple command line.
- Create a disk cache by adding the following line to your AUTOEXEC.BAT file (`XXXX` should equal about 25 percent of your available extended memory, in K):

  ```
  SMARTDRV.EXE XXXX 0
  ```

Running DOS 4 or Before on an 80386 or 80486-Based System

I hate to tell you this, but these older versions of DOS just don't provide any decent memory management—no matter how new or expensive your PC is! This means, of course, that you're left to third-party solutions such as QEMM-386 and 386MAX.

The Basic Setup

Consider these options for a basic 80386/80486-based system:

- Add as much extended memory to your system as possible; try to get your system to at least 4M total memory.
- Install a third-party memory manager designed specifically for 80386 and better PCs, such as QEMM-386 or 386MAX. You need to add a line to your CONFIG.SYS file to load the memory manager into memory.
- Create a disk cache using the driver supplied with your third-party memory manager. The cache should take up approximately 25 percent of your available expanded memory.
- Create a RAM disk using the driver supplied with your third-party memory manager. The RAM disk should take up approximately 25 percent of your available expanded memory.

If you prefer to use expanded memory (or have older DOS-based programs that use expanded memory), see the options presented for an 8088/8086-based system.

Running Windows

Your memory setup with Windows is quite different from your memory setup under DOS simply because several memory management tools come packaged with Windows at no extra charge. In particular, you now have access to HIMEM.SYS, SMARTDRV.EXE, and EMM386.EXE, all of which you can use in place of a third-party memory management solution.

Consider these options for an 80386/80486-based system running Windows:

- Add as much extended memory to your system as possible; try to get your system to at least 4M total memory.
- Add the following lines to your CONFIG.SYS file:

```
DEVICE=HIMEM.SYS
DEVICE=EMM386.EXE
```

- Load any other device drivers in your CONFIG.SYS file with the `DEVICE` command.
- Load any device drivers in your AUTOEXEC.BAT file normally with a simple command line.
- Create a disk cache by adding the following line to your AUTOEXEC.BAT file (`XXXX` should equal about 25 percent of your available extended memory, in K):

```
SMARTDRV.EXE XXXX 0
```

- Create virtual memory on your hard disk by opening the Windows Control Panel and double-clicking on the 386 Enhanced icon. When the 386 Enhanced dialog box appears, click on the Virtual Memory button to display the Virtual Memory dialog box. Click on the Change button and enter new settings for the amount of disk space you want to devote to virtual memory.

Wrapping It All Up

Let's face it, DOS memory management blew chunks before DOS 5. So, if you have an older version of DOS, your best bet is to forget everything I told you in this chapter and just upgrade to DOS 6. Trust me, it's the right thing to do.

31

The Best Memory Setups If You're Running Windows

If you're running Windows, there's just one key point to remember: free up as much extended memory as possible! Windows uses a lot of XMS, so give it as much as you can. And, in no circumstances should you use expanded memory—it's extended memory for Windows or it's nothing!

Yikes!

Because Windows uses free disk space as *virtual memory* on 80386- and 80486-based systems, it also helps to have about 5M of free disk space on your hard disk before you launch Windows. Anything less could freeze up your system.

Running Windows with DOS 6

MEMMAKER makes managing memory easy with DOS 6. You should use MEMMAKER's Custom Setup option to optimize your system for use with Windows. MEMMAKER should also sense the presence of Windows and ask you some basic questions about your system before it does its thing. See Chapter 23, "Working with DOS 6 Memory Management Tools," for more details on how to run MEMMAKER.

Remember, you can't run Windows from an 8088/8086 PC. So if you have an 80286 or better PC, consider these options to optimize your Windows memory usage:

- Add as much extended memory to your system as possible; try to get your system to at least 4M total memory.
- If you have at least a 386, run MEMMAKER using the Custom Setup. Answer the questions on the Advanced options screen as follows:

  Specify which drivers and TSRs to include in optimization? (No.)

  Scan the upper memory area aggressively? (Yes.)

  Optimize upper memory for use with Windows? (Yes, if you're using DOS programs as well as Windows programs; No, if you're using Windows programs exclusively.)

Use monochrome region (B000-BFFF) for running programs? (Yes, if you have an EGA or VGA monitor; No, if you have a SuperVGA or monochrome monitor.)

Keep current EMS386 memory exclusions and inclusions? (No.)

Move Extended BIOS Data Area from conventional to upper memory? (Yes.)

- If you have an 80286 system, be sure the following lines are present in your CONFIG.SYS file in the following order; if they (or some variation) are not there, add them:

```
DEVICE=HIMEM.SYS
DOS=HIGH
```

- If you have an 80386/80486 system, be sure the following lines are present in your CONFIG.SYS file in the following order; if they (or some variation) are not there, add them:

```
DEVICE=HIMEM.SYS
DEVICE=EMM386.EXE NOEMS
DOS=HIGH, UMB
```

- Load any other device drivers in your CONFIG.SYS file with the `DEVICEHIGH` command (80386/80486 systems) or the `DEVICE` command (80286 systems).
- Load any device drivers in your AUTOEXEC.BAT file with the `LOADHIGH` command (80386/80486 systems) or normally with a simple command line (80286 systems).
- If you have an 80286-based system, create a disk cache by adding the following line to your AUTOEXEC.BAT file:

```
SMARTDRV.EXE
```

- If you have an 80386/80486-based system, create a disk cache by adding the following line to your AUTOEXEC.BAT file:

```
LOADHIGH=SMARTDRV.EXE
```

- Change the BUFFERS, FILES, FCBS (if present), and STACKS statements in your CONFIG.SYS file to read:

```
BUFFERS=10,0
FILES=20
FCBS=1,0
STACKS=0,0
```

- If you have an 80386/80486-based system, create virtual memory on your hard disk by opening the Windows Control Panel and double-clicking on the 386 Enhanced icon. When the 386 Enhanced dialog box appears, click on the Virtual Memory button to display the Virtual Memory dialog box. Click on the Change button and enter new settings for the amount of disk space you want to devote to virtual memory.

Running Windows with DOS 5

DOS 5 was the first version of DOS truly optimized for Windows use. Most of the optimization involves the key memory management tools that allow you to easily access the HMA, UMBs, and extended memory.

Because you can't run Windows on an 8088/8086 PC, let's look at the options for higher-level systems:

- Add as much extended memory to your system as possible; try to get your system to at least 4M total memory.
- If you're running an 80286-based system, add the following lines to your CONFIG.SYS file in the following order:

```
DEVICE=HIMEM.SYS
DOS=HIGH
```

- If you're running an 80386/80486 system, add the following lines to your CONFIG.SYS file in the following order:

```
DEVICE=HIMEM.SYS
DEVICE=EMM386.EXE NOEMS
DOS=HIGH, UMB
```

- Load any other device drivers in your CONFIG.SYS file with the `DEVICEHIGH` command (80386/80486 systems) or the `DEVICE` command (80286 systems).
- Load any device drivers in your AUTOEXEC.BAT file with the `LOADHIGH` command (80386/80486 systems) or normally with a simple command line (80286 systems).
- If you have an 80286-based system, create a disk cache by adding the following line to your AUTOEXEC.BAT file (`XXXX` should equal about 25 percent of your available extended memory, in K):

```
SMARTDRV.EXE XXXX 0
```

- If you have an 80386/80486 system, create a disk cache by adding the following line to your AUTOEXEC.BAT file (`XXXX` should equal about 25 percent of your available extended memory, in K):

```
LOADHIGH=SMARTDRV.EXE XXXX 0
```

- Change the `BUFFERS`, `FILES`, `FCBS` (if present), and `STACKS` statements in your CONFIG.SYS file to read:

```
BUFFERS=10,0
FILES=20
FCBS=1,0
STACKS=0,0
```

- If you're running an 80386/80486 machine, create virtual memory on your hard disk by opening the Windows Control Panel and double-clicking on the 386 Enhanced icon. When the 386 Enhanced dialog box appears, click on the Virtual Memory button to display the Virtual Memory dialog box. Click on the Change button and enter new settings for the amount of disk space you want to devote to virtual memory.

Running Windows with DOS 4 or Before

Windows runs okay with DOS 4, although you can't optimize things anywhere near the degree you can with DOS 5 or 6. Because older versions of DOS actually include few memory management tools, you need to use the HIMEM.SYS, SMARTDRV.EXE, and EMM386.EXE files included with Windows.

Remember that you can only run Windows with an 80286 or better PC. The recommended options are pretty much the same whether you're running an 80286, 80386, or 80486 machine:

- Add as much extended memory to your system as possible; try to get your system to at least 4M total memory.
- Add the following line to your CONFIG.SYS file:

  ```
  DEVICE=HIMEM.SYS
  ```

- If you have an 80386/80486 system, add the following line directly below the HIMEM.SYS command:

  ```
  DEVICE=EMM386.EXE
  ```

- Load any other device drivers in your CONFIG.SYS file with the `DEVICE` command.
- Load any device drivers in your AUTOEXEC.BAT file normally with a simple command line.
- Create a disk cache by adding the following line to your AUTOEXEC.BAT file (`XXXX` should equal about 25 percent of your available extended memory, in K):

  ```
  SMARTDRV.EXE XXXX 0
  ```

- If you're running an 80386/80486 machine, create virtual memory on your hard disk by opening the Windows Control Panel and double-clicking on the 386 Enhanced icon. When the 386 Enhanced dialog box appears, click on the Virtual Memory button to display the Virtual Memory dialog box. Click on the Change button and enter new settings for the amount of disk space you want to devote to virtual memory.

Wrapping It All Up

Well, that wraps up this chapter on Windows—and the entire book! I hope you learned what you needed to know to better manage your system's memory and that your system is now running more efficiently than ever.

Remember, though, just because you're done with this book doesn't mean you're completely done with managing the memory on your system. You may wish to change your setup at some future date; you may install a new program (or operating system) that has different memory requirements; or you may decide to add more memory to your system.

If any of these scenarios occur, you'll need to thumb through this book once again. So keep it handy—you never know when you'll need to remember something about memory!

A

Glossary of Memory Management Terms

386MAX

A third-party memory management program from Qualitas designed for 80386- and 80486-based systems.

8088/8086

An older, slower Intel microprocessor (CPU).

80286

A slightly newer and faster Intel microprocessor (CPU) than the 8088/8086 chips.

80386

A very popular, moderately fast Intel microprocessor (CPU) faster than an 80286 but not as fast as an 80486.

80486

As of this writing, Intel's newest and fastest microprocessor (CPU).

Access time

The amount of time it takes to access one bit of data; memory access is measured in nanoseconds (ns).

Address

A specific location in memory.

AUTOEXEC.BAT

One of the two key system files used by DOS to configure your system on startup; many memory management commands can be added to this file.

Backfill

The process of filling up spare conventional memory (to the 640K limit) with excess expanded memory.

Bank

No, not something you keep money in. In the memory world, a bank is a collection of sockets found on your system unit's motherboard used to hold multiple RAM chips.

BIOS

Basic input/output system. A set of routines stored in a ROM chip that your system uses to start itself when power is turned on.

Bit

A binary digit, the smallest amount of information a computer can handle. Eight bits make a byte.

Block

A contiguous area of memory.

BlueMAX

A third-party memory management program from Qualitas designed for 80386- and 80486-based IBM PS/2 computers.

Boot

When you start your PC, you "boot" it.

Boot disk

A disk that contains hidden system files necessary to boot your computer.

Buffer

A disk buffer is an area of memory set aside to temporarily store information from your hard disk.

BUFFERS

A statement placed in your CONFIG.SYS file that sets the number of disk buffers.

Byte

Eight bits.

Cache

Temporary storage.

Chip

A small transistorized device that processes electronic signals.

CHKDSK

A DOS command used to display available conventional memory.

CMOS

A nonvolatile chip on your system's motherboard that stores essential system startup information.

CONFIG.SYS

One of the two key system files (along with AUTOEXEC.BAT) used by DOS to configure your system on startup; many memory management commands can be added to this file.

Conventional memory

The first 640K of RAM on your system.

CPU

Central processing unit. The microprocessor that controls the operation of your system.

DEVICE

A DOS command used to load device drivers into memory, used in the CONFIG.SYS file.

Device driver

A small file that, when loaded into system memory, controls a particular device (such as a printer or video card).

DEVICEHIGH

A DOS command used to load device drivers into upper memory, used in the CONFIG.SYS file.

DIP

Dual in-line package, a type of RAM chip.

Disk

A physical medium for long-term data storage.

Disk cache

A temporary storage area created in your system's memory for frequently accessed data.

DOS

Disk operating system. The software that manages your entire computer system. Microsoft sells MS-DOS; the version that IBM markets is called PC DOS.

DR DOS

A third-party version of DOS distributed by Novell.

DRAM

Dynamic random access memory, a type of memory chip.

Driver

See device driver.

Dynamic RAM

See DRAM.

EMM386.EXE

The memory manager driver included with DOS 5 and 6, manages access to upper memory.

EMS

See extended memory.

Expanded memory

Memory that resides outside your system's normal address space, accessed through a page frame in upper memory.

Extended memory

Any memory above 1M on your system.

FCBS

A statement placed in your CONFIG.SYS file that sets the number of file control blocks.

File control blocks

An area of RAM used to keep track of open files.

FILES

A statement placed in your CONFIG.SYS file that sets the number of file handles.

Hidden files

Two special files that work with your system's BIOS to boot your computer when its switch is turned on.

High memory area

The first 640K of extended memory.

HIMEM.SYS

The DOS device driver used to access the HMA.

HMA

See High Memory Area

Interleave

The process of creating two small groups of memory addresses instead of one large group; interleaved memory is faster to access than noninterleaved memory.

Kilobyte

One thousand bytes, abbreviated as "K."

LH

An abbreviation for the `LOADHIGH` command.

LIM

The Lotus-Intel-Microsoft expanded memory specification.

LOADHIGH

A DOS command used to load device drivers and programs into upper memory, used in the AUTOEXEC.BAT file.

Lower memory

Another term for *conventional memory*.

Manifest

A memory analysis utility from Quarterdeck included with QEMM-386.

Megabyte

One million bytes, abbreviated as "M."

MEM

A DOS command that analyzes your system's memory usage and creates an on-screen report.

MEMMAKER

A DOS utility program that automatically optimizes your system's memory usage.

Memory

Nonphysical, temporary data storage.

Microprocessor

An electronic chip that controls your system's operation, also called a *CPU*.

Motherboard

The main circuit board in your computer's system unit.

MOVE'EM

A third-party memory management program from Qualitas designed for 8088/8086- and 80286-based systems.

MS-DOS

The version of DOS developed by Microsoft.

Nanosecond

One billionth of a second, abbreviated as "ns."

Page frame

An unused area of upper memory used as a gateway to expanded memory.

Parameter

An optional part of a DOS command.

Protected mode

An operating mode available with 80286, 80386, and 80486 microprocessors that permits access to memory above 1M.

QEMM-386

A third-party memory management program from Quarterdeck designed for 80386- and 80486-based systems.

QRAM

A third-party memory management program from Quarterdeck designed for 8088/8086- and 80286-based systems.

RAM

See random access memory.

RAM disk

A virtual disk created in RAM.

RAMDRIVE.SYS

The device driver used in DOS 5 and 6 to create a RAM disk in system memory.

Random access memory

Memory that can be both written to and read from.

Read-only memory

Memory that can only be read from, not written to.

Real mode

The operating mode of 80286 and above microprocessors that is compatible with 8088/8086 chips, can only access 1M RAM.

ROM

See read-only memory.

SIMM

Single in-line memory module, a type of RAM chip.

SIP

Single in-line package, a type of RAM chip.

SMARTDrive

A DOS program that creates a disk cache in system memory.

SMARTDRV.EXE

The version of SMARTDrive included with DOS 6 and Windows, loads via the AUTOEXEC.BAT file.

SMARTDRV.SYS

The version of SMARTDrive included with DOS 5, loads via the CONFIG.SYS file.

SRAM

Static random access memory. A type of memory chip.

Stack area

An area of memory used to track interrupts.

STACKS

A statement placed in your CONFIG.SYS file that controls your system's stack area.

Static RAM

See SRAM.

System files

The two files used to configure your system on startup: AUTOEXEC.BAT and CONFIG.SYS.

System unit

The main part of your computer (the big beige box) that contains your motherboard and various cards.

Terminate-and-stay-resident program

See TSR.

Third-party program

An alternative, from a separate software publisher, to a utility built into your operating system.

TSR

Terminate-and-stay-resident program. A utility program that loads itself into memory, laying dormant until called into action by you, the user.

UMB

Upper memory block, a contiguous area of upper memory.

Upper memory

The area of memory between 640K and 1M.

Upper memory block

See UMB.

VDISK.SYS

The device driver used in DOS 4 and earlier versions to create a RAM disk in system memory.

Video RAM

Random access memory specifically devoted to your video card and driver.

Virtual disk

A disk that isn't a disk; virtual disks are normally created in memory.

Virtual memory

Memory that isn't memory; virtual memory is normally created on a disk.

VRAM

See video RAM.

Wait state

The number of clock cycles that your CPU must wait while a RAM chip refreshes itself.

Windows

An operating environment from Microsoft that places a graphical user interface on top of DOS.

XMS

See expanded memory.

ZIP

Zigzag in-line package, a type of RAM chip.

B

DOS 6 Memory Management Commands and Drivers

This appendix lists all applicable commands, utilities, and device drivers used for memory management with DOS 6. Any optional parameters/switches are listed in parentheses; everything else is mandatory. If there are multiposition toggle switches, the switches are separated by vertical bars (¦).

Memory Management Commands and Utilities

BUFFERS

The BUFFERS statement, located in your CONFIG.SYS file, allocates memory for a specified number of disk buffers. The syntax for this statement is as follows:

```
BUFFERS=n[,m]
```

The parameters for this statement are as follows:

- n — Specifies the number of disk buffers in a range from 1 through 99.
- m — Specifies the number of buffers in the secondary buffer cache in a range from 0 through 8.

A typical buffer statement might look like this:

```
BUFFERS=10,0
```

CHKDSK

The CHKDSK command, typed at the DOS prompt, checks the status of a disk and displays information about your system's use of conventional memory. The syntax for this command is:

```
CHKDSK [DRIVE:][[PATH]FILENAME] [/F] [/V]
```

The parameters for this command are as follows:

DRIVE	Specifies the drive you wish to check.
PATH	Specifies the directory path of any specific file you wish to check.
FILENAME	Specifies a specific file you wish to check for fragmentation.
/F	This switch, when specified, automatically fixes errors on the specified disk.
/V	This switch, when specified, displays the name of each file in every directory as the disk is checked.

To use CHKDSK to check conventional memory usage, type the following command (not using any optional parameters):

```
CHKDSK
```

DEVICE

The DEVICE command, located in your CONFIG.SYS file, is used to load device drivers into memory. The syntax for this command is:

```
DEVICE=[drive:][path]filename [x]
```

The parameters for this command are as follows:

DRIVE	Specifies the drive where the device driver resides.
PATH	Specifies the directory path where the device driver resides.
FILENAME	Specifies the name of the device driver.
X	Specifies any command-line parameters required by the device driver.

A typical DEVICE command might look like the following:

```
DEVICE=C:\DOS\ANSI.SYS
```

DEVICEHIGH

The DEVICEHIGH command, located in your CONFIG.SYS file, is identical to the DEVICE command, except that it loads the device driver into your system's upper memory area. The syntax for this command is:

```
DEVICEHIGH=[drive:][path]filename [x]
```

Parameters are identical to those of the DEVICE command. A typical DEVICEHIGH command might look like this:

```
DEVICEHIGH=C:\DOS\ANSI.SYS
```

DOS

The DOS command, located in your CONFIG.SYS file, is used to load DOS into the high memory area (HMA) and/or create upper memory blocks (UMBs). The syntax for this command is:

```
DOS=[HIGH¦LOW][UMB¦NOUMB]
```

The parameters for this command are as follows:

HIGH¦LOW	Specifies whether DOS should (HIGH) or should not (LOW) load part of itself into the HMA
UMB¦NOUMB	Specifies whether DOS should (UMB) or should not (NOUMB) create UMBs.

To load DOS into HMA and create UMBs, the command looks like this:

```
DOS=HIGH,UMB
```

FCBS

The `FCBS` statement, located in your CONFIG.SYS file, allocates memory for a specified number of file control blocks (FCBs). The syntax for this statement is:

```
FCBS=x
```

The parameter for this statement is as follows:

`x`	Specifies the number of FCBs that DOS can have open at one time (in a range from 1 through 255). The default value is 4.

A typical `FCBS` statement might look like this:

```
FCBS=1
```

FILES

The `FILES` statement, located in your CONFIG.SYS file, allocates memory for a specified number of files. The syntax for this statement is:

```
FILES=x
```

The parameter for this statement is as follows:

`x`	Specifies the number of files that DOS can have open at one time (in a range from 8 through 255). The default value is 8.

A typical `FILES` statement might look like this:

```
FILES=20
```

LOADHIGH

The `LOADHIGH` command, located in your AUTOEXEC.BAT file, is used to load device drivers and programs into your system's upper memory area. The syntax for this command is:

```
LOADHIGH [DRIVE:][PATH]FILENAME [X]
```

The parameters for this command are as follows:

`DRIVE`	Specifies the drive where the device driver or program resides.
`PATH`	Specifies the directory path where the device driver or program resides.
`FILENAME`	Specifies the name of the device driver or program.
`X`	Specifies any command-line parameters required by the device driver or program.

PSST!

Note that you can abbreviate `LOADHIGH` as `LH`.

A typical `LOADHIGH` command might look like this:

```
LOADHIGH C:\DOS\SMARTDRV.EXE
```

MEM

The `MEM` command, typed at the DOS prompt, displays details of your system's memory use. The syntax for this command is:

```
MEM   [/C¦/D¦/F¦/M [MODULENAME]] [/P]
```

The optional switches for this command are as follows:

/C	The classify switch lists all programs that are currently loaded into memory.
/D	The debug switch lists all programs and internal drivers that are currently loaded into memory. The debug report shows each module's size, segment address, and type, in addition to normal MEM information.
/F	The free switch lists the free areas of conventional and upper memory.
/M	The module switch shows how a program module is currently using memory. If you use the /M switch, you have to specify which module (MODULENAME) you wish to examine.
MODULENAME	The name of the module you wish to examine with the /M switch.
/P	The page switch pauses the MEM report after each screen of output.

Yikes!

You cannot use the /C, /D, /F, or /M switches simultaneously.

To use MEM to display information about all programs currently in memory (and to pause after each screen of information), type the following:

```
MEM /C /P
```

MEMMAKER

MEMMAKER is a utility program that optimizes your system's use of memory. It edits your CONFIG.SYS and AUTOEXEC.BAT files to move device drivers and programs to upper memory, in the most efficient manner. The syntax to launch MEMMAKER is:

```
MEMMAKER [/B] [/BATCH] [/SWAP:DRIVE] [/T] [/UNDO] [/W:n,m]
```

PSST!  To use MEMMAKER you must have an 80386- or 80486-based system and extended memory.

The optional parameters for MEMMAKER are as follows:

`/B`	Displays MEMMAKER in black and white.
`/BATCH`	Runs MEMMAKER in batch mode. By taking only default actions at all prompts, you can run MEMMAKER unattended.
`/SWAP:[DRIVE]`	Specifies the letter of the drive `[DRIVE]` that was originally your startup disk drive. This switch is necessary only if the drive letter of your startup disk has changed since your computer started.
`/T`	Disables the detection of IBM Token-Ring networks.
`/UNDO`	Instructs MEMMAKER to undo its most recent changes.
`/W:n,m`	Specifies how much upper memory space to reserve for Windows translation buffers, where `n` is the size of the first region, and `m` is the size of the second region. By default, MEMMAKER does not reserve upper memory for Windows; this parameter can be manually adjusted within the MEMMAKER operation.

To run MEMMAKER in a normal fashion, without any optional parameters, type the following:

```
MEMMAKER
```

STACKS

The `STACKS` statement, located in your CONFIG.SYS file, allocates memory for a specified number of data control stacks to handle hardware interrupts. The syntax for this statement is:

```
STACKS=n,s
```

The parameters for this statement are as follows:

- `n` Specifies the number of stacks in a range from 8 through 64 (plus 0).
- `s` Specifies the size (in bytes) of each stack in a range from 32 through 512 (plus 0).

A typical `STACKS` statement might look like this:

```
STACKS=0,0
```

Memory Management Device Drivers

EMM386.EXE

The EMM386.EXE driver provides access to the upper memory area and uses extended memory to simulate expanded memory. This driver must be loaded by a `DEVICE` command in your CONFIG.SYS file. The syntax for loading EMM386.EXE is:

```
DEVICE=[DRIVE:][PATH]EMM386.EXE [ON¦OFF¦AUTO] [MEMORY]
[MIN=SIZE] [W=ON¦W=OFF] [NOEMS] [HIGHSCAN] [VERBOSE] [NOHI]
[NOMOVEXBDA] [ALTBOOT]
```

PSST! To use EMM386.EXE you must have an 80386- or 80486-based system and extended memory.

The parameters for this driver are as follows:

Parameter	Description
`DRIVE:`	Specifies the drive where EMM386.EXE resides.
`PATH`	Specifies the directory path where EMM386.EXE resides.
`ON¦OFF¦AUTO`	`ON` activates the EMM386 device driver. `OFF` suspends the EMM386 device driver. `AUTO` places the EMM386 device driver into automatic mode, where expanded memory and UMB support are enabled only when a program calls for it. The default value is `ON`.
`MEMORY`	Specifies the maximum amount of extended memory (in K) that the driver will provide as expanded memory (in the range of 64 to 32,768, or whatever the total amount of extended memory is installed on your system). The default value is the amount of free extended memory available.
`MIN=SIZE`	Specifies the minimum amount of extended memory (in K) that the driver will provide (in the range of 0 through the value of the `MEMORY` parameter). The default value is 256.
`W=ON¦W=OFF`	Enables (`ON`) or disables (`OFF`) support for the Weitek coprocessor. The default setting is `OFF`.
`NOEMS`	Provides access to the upper memory area while preventing access to expanded memory.

HIGHSCAN	Specifies that EMM386 use an additional check to determine the available amount of upper memory. Not necessary on most computers.
VERBOSE	Directs the driver to display status and error messages when loading.
NOHI	Prevents the driver from loading into the upper memory area.
NOMOVEXBDA	Prevents the driver from moving the extended BIOS into upper memory.
ALTBOOT	Specifies that the driver should use an alternate handler to restart your system when you press Ctrl+Alt+Del. Necessary only if your PC exhibits an unusual system when rebooting.

A typical EMM386.EXE command might look something like this:

```
DEVICE=C:\DOS\EMM386.EXE NOEMS
```

HIMEM.SYS

The HIMEM.SYS driver is an extended memory manager and provides access to your PC's high memory area (HMA). This driver must be loaded by a `DEVICE` command in your CONFIG.SYS file. The syntax for loading HIMEM.SYS is:

```
DEVICE=[DRIVE:][PATH]HIMEM.SYS [A20CONTROL:ON¦OFF]
➥[/CPULOCK:ON¦OFF] [/EISA] [/HMAMIN=m] [/NUMHANDLES=n]
➥[/MACHINE=x] [/SHADOWRAM:ON¦OFF] [/VERBOSE]
```

The parameters for this driver are as follows:

DRIVE:	Specifies the drive where HIMEM.SYS resides.
PATH	Specifies the directory path where HIMEM.SYS resides.

`/A20CONTROL:ON¦OFF`	Specifies whether the driver should (ON) or should not (OFF) take control of the A20 handler on the system. The default setting is ON.
`/CPUCLOCK:ON¦OFF`	Specifies whether the driver should (ON) or should not (OFF) affect the clock speed of your computer. The default setting is OFF.
`/EISA`	Specifies that the driver should allocate all available extended memory. This switch is necessary only on an EISA computer with more than 16M of memory.
`/HMAMIN=m`	Specifies how much memory (in K) an application must require before the driver loads it into the HMA (in the range of 0 to 63). The default value is 0.
`/NUMHANDLES=n`	Specifies the maximum number of extended memory block handles that can be used simultaneously (in the range of 1 to 128). The default value is 32.
`/MACHINE=X`	Specifies what type of computer you are using. See your DOS documentation for a complete list of machines and their corresponding numbers (X). In normal operation HIMEM.SYS can successfully detect the correct machine type.
`/SHADOWRAM:ON¦OFF`	Specifies whether shadow RAM (ROM code copied into RAM memory) should (ON) or should not (OFF) be enabled. The default is ON.
`/VERBOSE`	Directs the driver to display status and error messages when loading.

PSST!

In most cases, you won't need to specify any parameters for HIMEM.SYS. (Good thing, eh?)

A typical command to load this driver looks something like this:

```
DEVICE=C:\DOS\HIMEM.SYS
```

RAMDRIVE.SYS

The RAMDRIVE.SYS driver is used to create a RAM disk using your system's memory. This driver must be loaded by a `DEVICE` command in your CONFIG.SYS file. The syntax for loading RAMDRIVE.SYS is:

```
DEVICE[HIGH]=[DRIVE:][PATH]RAMDRIVE.SYS [DISKSIZE SECTORSIZE
[NUMENTRIES]] [/E¦/A]
```

PSST!

You can load this driver into either conventional memory (with the `DEVICE` command) or into UMB (with the `DEVICEHIGH` command).

The parameters for this driver are as follows:

`DRIVE:`	Specifies the drive where RAMDRIVE.SYS resides.
`PATH`	Specifies the directory path where RAMDRIVE.SYS resides.
`DISKSIZE`	Specifies how much memory (in K) to use for the RAM disk (in the range of 4 to 32,767). The default value is 64K.

`SECTORSIZE`	Specifies the disk sector size, in bytes. The size can be either 128, 256, or 512 bytes. The default value is 512 bytes.
`NUMENTRIES`	Limits the number of files and directories you can create in the root directory of the RAM drive (in the range of 2 to 1,024). The default value is 64 entries.
`/E`	Creates the RAM drive using extended memory.
`/A`	Creates the RAM drive using expanded memory.

The command to create a 2M RAM drive in extended memory (with the driver in UMBs and using all other default parameters) looks like this:

```
DEVICEHIGH=C:\DOS\RAMDRIVE.SYS 2048 /E
```

SMARTDRV.EXE

The SMARTDRV.EXE driver is used to create a disk cache using your system's memory. This driver must be loaded in your AUTOEXEC.BAT file. The syntax for loading SMARTDRV.EXE is:

```
[DRIVE:][PATH]SMARTDRV.EXE [[DRIVE[+¦-]X:] [/E:ELEMENTSIZE]
[INITCACHESIZE] [WINCACHESIZE] [/B:BUFFERSIZE] [/C] [/R] [/L]
[/V¦/Q] [/S]
```

PSST!

You can load this driver into either conventional memory or into UMB (with the `LOADHIGH` command).

The parameters for this driver are as follows:

`DRIVE:`	Specifies the drive where SMARTDRV.EXE resides.
`PATH`	Specifies the directory path where SMARTDRV.EXE resides.
`DRIVE+¦- X:`	Specifies the letter of the disk drive for which you want to create the disk cache. The plus sign (+) enables caching for the specified drive; the minus sign (-) disables caching. The `X:` is the specified drive; you can specify multiple drives. If you don't use this parameter, the driver caches all available hard disk drives.
`/E:ELEMENTSIZE`	Specifies the amount of cache that the driver moves at a time, in bytes. Valid values are 1,024, 2,048, 4,096, and 8,192. The default value is 8,192.
`INITCACHESIZE`	Specifies the size of the disk cache (in K) used for DOS applications. If this parameter is not specified, the driver sets the value according to how much memory is available on your system.
`WINCACHESIZE`	Specifies the size of the disk cache (in K) used for Windows. If this parameter is not specified, the driver sets the value according to how much memory is available on your system.
`/B:BUFFERSIZE`	Specifies the size of the read-ahead buffer (in K). The default value is 16K.
`/C`	Writes all caches information from memory to cached disks.
`/R`	Clears the contents of the existing cache and restarts the driver.

`/L` Prevents the driver from automatically loading into UMBs.

`/V|/Q` Instructs the driver either to (`/V`) or not to (`/Q`) display status and error messages when it starts.

`/S` Displays additional information about the status of the driver.

To create a disk cache in UMB of 4M for DOS applications and 2M for Windows, the command looks like this:

```
LOADHIGH C:\DOS\SMARTDRV.EXE 4096 2048
```

PSST! 

SMARTDRV.EXE automatically creates the disk cache in extended memory; you can't use SMARTDRV.EXE if you only have expanded memory.

C

DOS 5 Memory Management Commands and Drivers

This appendix lists all applicable commands, utilities, and device drivers used for memory management with DOS 5. Any optional parameters/switches are listed in parentheses; everything else is mandatory. If there are multi-position toggle switches, the switches are separated by vertical bars (¦).

Memory Management Commands and Utilities

BUFFERS

The BUFFERS statement, located in your CONFIG.SYS file, allocates memory for a specified number of disk buffers. The syntax for this statement is:

```
BUFFERS=n[,m]
```

The parameters for this statement are as follows:

- n — Specifies the number of disk buffers (in a range from 1 through 99).
- m — Specifies the number of buffers in the secondary buffer cache (in a range from 0 through 8).

A typical buffer statement might look like this:

```
BUFFERS=10,0
```

CHKDSK

The CHKDSK command, typed at the DOS prompt, checks the status of a disk and displays information about your system's use of conventional memory. The syntax for this command is:

```
CHKDSK [DRIVE:][[PATH]FILENAME] [/F] [/V]
```

The parameters for this command are as follows:

`DRIVE`	Specifies the drive you wish to check.
`PATH`	Specifies the directory path of any specific file you wish to check.
`FILENAME`	Specifies a specific file you wish to check for fragmentation.
`/F`	This switch, when specified, automatically fixes errors on the specified disk.
`/V`	This switch, when specified, displays the name of each file in every directory as the disk is checked.

To use `CHKDSK` to check conventional memory usage, type the following command (not using any optional parameters):

```
CHKDSK
```

DEVICE

The `DEVICE` command, located in your CONFIG.SYS file, is used to load device drivers into memory. The syntax for this command is:

```
DEVICE=[drive:][path]filename [x]
```

The parameters for this command are as follows:

`DRIVE`	Specifies the drive where the device driver resides.
`PATH`	Specifies the directory path where the device driver resides.
`FILENAME`	Specifies the name of the device driver.
`X`	Specifies any command-line parameters required by the device driver.

A typical DEVICE command might look like this:

```
DEVICE=C:\DOS\ANSI.SYS
```

DEVICEHIGH

The DEVICEHIGH command, located in your CONFIG.SYS file, is identical to the DEVICE command, except that it loads the device driver into your system's upper memory area. The syntax for this command is:

```
DEVICEHIGH=[drive:][path]filename [x]
```

Parameters are identical to those of the DEVICE command. A typical DEVICEHIGH command might look like this:

```
DEVICEHIGH=C:\DOS\ANSI.SYS
```

DOS

The DOS command, located in your CONFIG.SYS file, is used to load DOS into the high memory area (HMA) and/or create upper memory blocks (UMBs). The syntax for this command is:

```
DOS=[HIGH¦LOW][UMB¦NOUMB]
```

The parameters for this command are as follows:

HIGH¦LOW	Specifies whether DOS should (HIGH) or should not (LOW) load part of itself into the HMA.
UMB¦NOUMB	Specifies whether DOS should (UMB) or should not (NOUMB) create UMBs.

To load DOS into HMA and create UMBs, the command looks like this:

```
DOS=HIGH,UMB
```

FCBS

The `FCBS` statement, located in your CONFIG.SYS file, allocates memory for a specified number of file control blocks (FCBs). The syntax for this statement is:

```
FCBS=x
```

The parameter for this statement is as follows:

`x`	Specifies the number of FCBs that DOS can have open at one time (in a range from 1 through 255). The default value is 4.

A typical `FCBS` statement might look like this:

```
FCBS=1
```

FILES

The `FILES` statement, located in your CONFIG.SYS file, allocates memory for a specified number of files. The syntax for this statement is:

```
FILES=x
```

The parameter for this statement is as follows:

`x`	Specifies the number of files that DOS can have open at one time (in a range from 8 through 255). The default value is 8.

A typical `FILES` statement might look like this:

```
FILES=20
```

LOADHIGH

The `LOADHIGH` command, located in your AUTOEXEC.BAT file, is used to load device drivers and programs into your system's upper memory area. The syntax for this command is:

```
LOADHIGH [DRIVE:][PATH]FILENAME [X]
```

The parameters for this command are as follows:

DRIVE	Specifies the drive where the device driver or program resides.
PATH	Specifies the directory path where the device driver or program resides.
FILENAME	Specifies the name of the device driver or program.
X	Specifies any command-line parameters required by the device driver or program.

PSST!  Note that you can abbreviate `LOADHIGH` as `LH`.

A typical `LOADHIGH` command might look like this:

```
LOADHIGH C:\DOS\SMARTDRV.EXE
```

MEM

The `MEM` command, typed at the DOS prompt, displays details of your system's memory use. The syntax for this command is:

```
MEM    [/C|/D|/P]
```

The optional switches for this command are as follows:

- `/C` The classify switch lists all programs that are currently loaded into memory, along with more detailed memory information.
- `/D` The debug switch lists all programs and internal drivers that are currently loaded into memory, along with more detailed memory information.
- `/P` The program switch lists all programs loaded into memory.

Yikes!

Note that you cannot use the /C, /D, or /P switches simultaneously.

To use MEM to display detailed information about all programs currently in memory, type the following:

```
MEM /C
```

STACKS

The STACKS statement, located in your CONFIG.SYS file, allocates memory for a specified number of data control stacks to handle hardware interrupts. The syntax for this statement is:

```
STACKS=n,s
```

The parameters for this statement are as follows:

- `n` Specifies the number of stacks—in a range from 8 through 64 (plus 0).

`s`	Specifies the size (in bytes) of each stack—in a range from 32 through 512 (plus 0).

A typical `STACKS` statement might look like this:

```
STACKS=0,0
```

Memory Management Device Drivers

EMM386.EXE

The EMM386.EXE driver provides access to the upper memory area and uses extended memory to simulate expanded memory. This driver must be loaded by a `DEVICE` command in your CONFIG.SYS file. The syntax for loading EMM386.EXE is:

```
DEVICE=[DRIVE:][PATH]EMM386.EXE [ON¦OFF¦AUTO] [W=ON¦W=OFF]
[L=MINXMS] [A=ALTREGS] [H=HANDLES] [RAM] [NOEMS]
```

PSST!

To use EMM386.EXE you must have an 80386- or 80486-based system and extended memory.

The parameters for this driver are as follows:

`DRIVE:`	Specifies the drive where EMM386.EXE resides.
`PATH`	Specifies the directory path where EMM386.EXE resides.

`ON¦OFF¦AUTO`	`ON` activates the EMM386 device driver. `OFF` suspends the EMM386 device driver. `AUTO` places the EMM386 device driver into automatic mode, where expanded memory and UMB support is enabled only when a program calls for it. The default value is `ON`.
`W=ON¦W=OFF`	Enables (`ON`) or disables (`OFF`) support for the Weitek coprocessor.
`L=MINXMS`	Specifies the amount of extended memory (in K) that will still be available after you load the driver. The default value is 0.
`A=ALTREGS`	Specifies how many fast alternate register sets should be allocated to the driver (in the range from 0 to 254). The default value is 7.
`H=HANDLES`	Specifies how many handles the driver can use (in the range of 2 to 255). The default value is 64.
`RAM`	Provides access to both expanded memory and the upper memory area.
`uNOEMS`	Provides access to the upper memory area while preventing access to expanded memory.

A typical EMM386.EXE command might look something like this:

```
DEVICE=C:\DOS\EMM386.EXE NOEMS
```

HIMEM.SYS

The HIMEM.SYS driver is an extended memory manager and provides access to your PC's high memory area (HMA). This driver must be loaded by a `DEVICE` command in your CONFIG.SYS file. The syntax for loading HIMEM.SYS is:

```
DEVICE=[DRIVE:][PATH]HIMEM.SYS [A20CONTROL:ON¦OFF]
[/CPULOCK:ON¦OFF] [/HMAMIN=m] [/NUMHANDLES=n] [/MACHINE=x]
[/SHADOWRAM:ON¦OFF]
```

The parameters for this driver are as follows:

`DRIVE:`	Specifies the drive where HIMEM.SYS resides.
`PATH`	Specifies the directory path where HIMEM.SYS resides.
`/A20CONTROL:ON¦OFF`	Specifies whether the driver should (`ON`) or should not (`OFF`) take control of the A20 handler on the system. The default setting is ON.
`/CPUCLOCK:ON¦OFF`	Specifies whether the driver should (`ON`) or should not (`OFF`) affect the clock speed of your computer. The default setting is `OFF`.
`/HMAMIN=m`	Specifies how much memory (in K) an application must require before the driver loads it into the HMA (in the range of 0 to 63). The default value is 0.
`/NUMHANDLES=n`	Specifies the maximum number of extended-memory block handles that can be used simultaneously (in the range of 1 to 128). The default value is 32.
`/MACHINE=X`	Specifies what type of computer you are using. See your DOS documentation for a complete list of machines and their corresponding numbers (`X`). In normal operation, HIMEM.SYS can successfully detect the correct machine type.

`/SHADOWRAM:ON¦OFF`	Specifies whether shadow RAM (ROM code copied into RAM memory) should (`ON`) or should not (`OFF`) be enabled. The default is `ON`.

PSST! In most cases, you won't need to specify any parameters for HIMEM.SYS. (Good thing, eh?)

A typical command to load this driver looks something like this:

```
DEVICE=C:\DOS\HIMEM.SYS
```

RAMDRIVE.SYS

The RAMDRIVE.SYS driver is used to create a RAM disk using your system's memory. This driver must be loaded by a `DEVICE` command in your CONFIG.SYS file. The syntax for loading RAMDRIVE.SYS is:

```
DEVICE[HIGH]=[DRIVE:][PATH]RAMDRIVE.SYS [DISKSIZE SECTORSIZE
[NUMENTRIES]] [/E¦/A]
```

PSST! You can load this driver into either conventional memory (with the `DEVICE` command) or into UMB (with the command).

The parameters for this driver are as follows:

`DRIVE:`	Specifies the drive where RAMDRIVE.SYS resides.
`PATH`	Specifies the directory path where RAMDRIVE.SYS resides.

`DISKSIZE`	Specifies how much memory (in K) to use for the RAM disk (in the range of 4 to 32,767). The default value is 64K.
`SECTORSIZE`	Specifies the disk sector size, in bytes. The size can be either 128, 256, or 512 bytes. The default value is 512 bytes.
`NUMENTRIES`	Limits the number of files and directories you can create in the root directory of the RAM drive (in the range of 2 to 1,024). The default value is 64 entries.
`/E`	Creates the RAM drive using extended memory.
`/A`	Creates the RAM drive using expanded memory.

The command to create a 2M RAM drive in extended memory (with the driver in UMBs and using all other default parameters) looks like this:

```
DEVICEHIGH=C:\DOS\RAMDRIVE.SYS 2048 /E
```

SMARTDRV.EXE

The SMARTDRV.SYS driver is used to create a disk cache using your system's memory. This driver must be loaded in your CONFIG.SYS file. The syntax for loading SMARTDRV.SYS is:

```
DEVICE[HIGH]=[DRIVE:][PATH]SMARTDRV.SYS [INITCACHESIZE]
[MINCACHESIZE] /A
```

PSST!

You can load this driver into either conventional memory (with the `DEVICE` command) or into UMB (with the `DEVICEHIGH` command).

The parameters for this driver are as follows:

`DRIVE:`	Specifies the drive where SMARTDRV.SYS resides.
`PATH`	Specifies the directory path where SMARTDRV.SYS resides.
`INITCACHESIZE`	Specifies the size of the disk cache (in K) used for DOS applications (in the range of 128 to 8,192). The default value is 256K.
`MINCACHESIZE`	Specifies the minimum size of the disk cache (in K); generally used only if you're running Windows. If this parameter is not specified, there is no minimum cache size.
`/A`	Creates the disk cache in expanded memory. If this switch is not set, the disk cache is created in extended memory.

To create an extended-memory disk cache in UMB of 4M for DOS with a minimum cache of 2M for Windows, the command looks like this:

```
DEVICEHIGH=C:\DOS\SMARTDRV.SYS 4096 2048
```

D

Windows Memory Management Options

This appendix lists (briefly) the various memory management options and topics applicable to Windows. For a more detailed explanation of this topic, see Chapter 25, "Managing Windows Memory."

Device Drivers

Windows comes with these memory-related device drivers:

- EMM386.EXE. Load EMM386.EXE in your CONFIG.SYS file to provide access to the upper memory area.
- HIMEM.SYS. Load HIMEM.SYS in your CONFIG.SYS file to provide access to extended memory.
- SMARTDRV.EXE. Load SMARTDRV.EXE in your AUTOEXEC.BAT file and create a disk cache about one-quarter the size of your available extended memory.

Disk Cache Use

Windows needs a disk cache to run effectively. The SMARTDRV.EXE driver is recommended because it is optimized to work better with Windows than other caching programs.

DOS Program Operation

If you intend to use DOS programs from within Windows, you need to create a *program information file* by using the PIF Editor (located in the Main program group in the Windows Program Manager). Of the many settings available in a PIF file, the ones shown in Table D.1 are of particular importance to memory management.

Table D.1. PIF Options.

Option	*Description*
Video Memory	The higher the graphics mode selected, the more memory Windows sets aside for graphics use of this application.

Option	*Description*
Memory Requirements	Determines how Windows assigns conventional memory to your DOS application. The KB Required sets the minimum amount of memory assigned to the application; the KB Desired sets the maximum amount of memory available to the application.
EMS Memory	Determines the expanded memory allocation for your DOS application.
XMS Memory	Determines the extended memory allocation for your DOS allocation.
EMS Memory Locked	(Available as an Advanced option.) Prevents any expanded memory used by this application to be swapped to the hard disk as virtual memory.
Uses High Memory Area	(Available as an Advanced option.) Allows the application to use the HMA, if available.
XMS Memory Locked	(Available as an Advanced option.) Prevents any extended memory used by this application to be swapped to the hard disk as virtual memory.
Lock Application Memory	(Available as an Advanced option.) Prevents the application from releasing any conventional memory used when data is swapped to the hard disk as virtual memory.

DOS Version

DOS 6 is the recommended version of DOS for Windows use. It is better optimized for use with Windows than any previous version of DOS.

MEMMAKER Custom Setup

When you run MEMMAKER, let it know that you're running Windows. Then run the Custom Setup and answer the questions on the Advanced options screen as follows:

- **Specify which drivers and TSRs to include in optimization?** (No.)
- **Scan the upper memory area aggressively?** (Yes.)
- **Optimize upper memory for use with Windows?** (Yes, if you're using DOS programs as well as Windows programs; No, if you're using Windows programs exclusively.)
- **Use monochrome region (B000-BFFF) for running programs?** (Yes, if you have an EGA or VGA monitor; No, if you have a SuperVGA or monochrome monitor.)
- **Keep current EMS386 memory exclusions and inclusions?** (No.)
- **Move Extended BIOS Data Area from conventional to upper memory?** (Yes.)

Memory Use

Windows needs a minimum of 2M total memory to start. A minimum of 4M is recommended for efficient operation. Windows uses extended memory; it cannot access expanded memory. If some of your programs need expanded memory, Windows simulates whatever is needed if you run the program from within Windows. Windows reserves all available extended memory for its own use and all available conventional memory for any DOS programs you run from within Windows. For these reasons, use UMBs and the HMA efficiently; load DOS and any other drivers and programs high, if possible.

Operating Modes

Windows 3.1 has two separate operating modes. The default operating mode is called the Enhanced mode; it requires the most memory to operate. The lower-performance Standard mode (available by typing `WIN /S` at the DOS prompt) uses less memory, but limits Windows functionality—including the ability to run DOS programs from within Windows.

RAM Disk Use

A RAM disk is not necessary with Windows; it's preferable to use a disk cache and allocate the rest of your extended memory for Windows to use on its own.

System Resources

Windows counts both RAM and virtual memory as available memory. To view Windows combined RAM/disk memory, pull down the **H**elp menu in the Windows Program Manager and select the **A**bout Program Manager option. When the About Program Manager dialog box appears, you see a display of Free Memory and Free System Resources (which includes memory, disk space, and other items).

Unreleased Memory

When a Windows program is closed, its reserved memory is supposed to be released. However, some programs don't release all their memory when they close. To free up this unreleased memory, you have to exit and restart Windows.

Virtual Memory

Windows uses free space on your hard disk to simulate normal random access memory. This *virtual memory* speeds up Windows operation under high load situations. To change your virtual memory setup, open the Windows Control Panel and double-click on the 386 Enhanced icon. When the 386 Enhanced dialog box appears, click on the Virtual Memory button to display the Virtual Memory dialog box. To change your virtual memory settings, click on the Change button; the Virtual Memory dialog box enlarges to include a New Settings area where you can change the drive used for virtual memory, the *type* of virtual memory (permanent is preferred), and the size of the virtual memory area.

E

Five Tips to Optimize Hard Disk Efficiency

Yeah, I know, this is supposed to be a book about memory storage, not about disk storage. But the two both do kind of the same thing—in their own ways:

your hard disk as *virtual memory*, and you're probably using some memory as a *virtual disk*. So let's look at five easy tips to help you maximize the use of your hard disk.

Tip 1: Defragment Your Hard Disk

Hard disks are kind of like memory in that new data is written to the medium in the order it appears. Big data chunks and little data chunks coexist side-by-side (track-by-track, actually) on your hard disk. Older data appears before newer data, that is, until older data is *erased* from your disk. Then the space it formerly occupied is made available for new data.

So, new data can be placed at the "end" of your disk or in the "middle"—in place of older data that has been erased. Problems arise when your newer data doesn't take up as much space as the erased older data, leaving empty "holes" on your disk. Often these "holes" are too small to hold complete chunks of data.

DOS, in its infinite wisdom (ha!), sometimes sees a lot of these small empty "holes" on your hard disk and tries to use them by chopping up data chunks and spreading them among several "holes." Yup, that's right, a single data chunk can be *fragmented* throughout your entire hard disk. This, as you can imagine, makes it more difficult for DOS to find and access data, thus slowing down your computer's operation.

For this reason, from time to time you need to get rid of empty "holes" and rearrange your disk so that like data chunks occupy contiguous areas on your disk. This process is called *defragmenting* (which sounds a lot more technical than "deholing"), and really speeds up your hard disk performance.

PSST! It's a good idea to do some housekeeping on your hard disk before you defragment it. Go through all your directories and subdirectories and delete unused and unwanted files, freeing up disk space before you defragment your disk. Whenever you delete a lot of files (thus freeing up more discontiguous fragments), you probably need to reun-fragment your hard disk!

Prior to DOS 6, you had to buy a third-party utility package (such as PC Tools Deluxe or The Norton Utilities) to obtain a defragmenter utility. DOS 6, however, includes its own disk defragmenter, called Defragmenter. (Imaginative name, eh? I would have preferred "Deholer!")

Skip This, It's Technical!

Actually, Defragmenter is a version of the Speedisk defragmenter utility included with The Norton Utilities, and it is licensed by Microsoft from Symantec.

To run Defragmenter, you need to be at the DOS prompt. (You can't run Defragmenter from another operating environment such as Windows.) Just type the following command:

```
DEFRAG
```

When Defragmenter is done, your disk is more orderly and your system runs faster! It's a good idea to defragment your hard disk once a month or so, or more if you frequently erase a large number of files.

Tip 2: Create Virtual Memory on Your Hard Disk (for Windows)

If you're running Windows, you want to create an area on your hard disk for Windows to use as *virtual memory*. Virtual memory is nothing more than disk space that Windows can use as extra memory if it needs to. So, if Windows is running some very large applications (or working with very large data files), it can use this area on your disk as temporary overflow memory.

Skip This, It's Technical!

Virtual memory can only be created on PCs with 80386 or 80486 CPUs. Note, however, that virtual memory on your hard disk is much slower than true RAM-based memory.

When you first install Windows, you're prompted to create virtual memory on your hard disk. You can also create (or change) virtual memory after installation by double-clicking on the 386 Enhanced icon in the Windows Control Panel. (See Chapter 25, "Managing Windows Memory," for detailed instructions on how to create a virtual memory area.)

When you're done, you've created a protected area of your hard disk to be used exclusively by Windows as virtual memory. This lets you do things you might not have had enough memory to do—without having to add extra memory to your system!

Tip 3: Compress the Data on Your Hard Disk

Hard disks, as big as they are (in terms of megabytes of available storage), seem to fill up too fast. No matter how big your hard disk is, it's just too easy to find enough programs and utilities and clip art files and games and documents and other stuff to fill it to the brim. So what do you do when your hard disk isn't big enough? Simple—make it bigger.

Now, that sounds like some magician's trick, doesn't it? Well, there are ways to take your existing hard disk and make it store more data. This is done by *compressing* the data on your hard disk so that it occupies less space. This compression actually stores your data in a different, more compressed file format. In this special format, you can cram more data onto your hard disk than with the normal DOS file formats.

Compressing the data on your hard disk is actually very easy and very safe. The compression program handles all the file conversions on the fly, so you never even know that you're using compressed data!

To compress your data, you need a special compression program. Prior to DOS 6, you had to buy a third-party compression package (such as Stacker) to compress your hard disk. DOS 6, however, includes its own compression program called DoubleSpace. After you set up DoubleSpace, your hard disk will have anywhere from 50 to 100 percent more available disk space. (That's right—you can double your hard disk's capacity with DoubleSpace!)

To run DoubleSpace, you need to be at the DOS prompt. (You can't run DoubleSpace from another operating environment, such as Windows.) Just type the following command:

```
DBLSPACE
```

See your DOS 6 documentation for full instructions on setting up and using DoubleSpace.

When DoubleSpace is done, your disk is now compressed—and you have a lot more free disk space!

Tip 4: Create an Efficient Directory Structure

When you're using your hard disk, it's best if you know where all your files are. This argues in favor of creating a well-organized directory structure. (The alternative is just to dump everything into one huge directory, which is not only inefficient, but also impractical—DOS actually imposes a limit on how many files you can create in a single directory!)

Naturally, most programs install into their own unique directories, but you have control over where everything else on your hard disk goes. You should organize your hard disk so that it is efficient, so that it makes sense, and so that you can quickly find any files you want to find.

If you want to learn more about creating directories, go out and buy Alan Simpson's *DOS Secrets Unleashed*, a truly monster DOS book from Sams.

You need to create a directory structure that makes sense to you. I recommend creating a separate directory for all your data; I call mine DATA. (See, I can be just as imaginative as the folks at Microsoft!) From this directory you can create subdirectories for different types of data files. For example, you can create a subdirectory called 123 for your 1-2-3 spreadsheets, EXCEL for your Excel spreadsheets, WINWORD for your Word for Windows documents, and so on:

```
C:
¦------   DATA
          ¦------123
          ¦------EXCEL
          ¦------WINWORD
```

Another useful directory to create is a UTILITY directory. I use my UTILITY directory as kind of a garbage dump where I toss all the odd DOS, Windows, and disk utilities that come my way. I also like a directory called WORK, where I store all the files I bring home from work.

The point is, you need to create a directory structure that makes sense to you. If you can't understand it, no one can—which means you'll never be able to find the files you need!

Tip 5: Set Up Your AUTOEXEC.BAT File Properly

An organized directory structure will help you find your files on your hard disk. But unless DOS can also find your files, you have some major problems!

There is one command in your AUTOEXEC.BAT file that helps DOS find the most important files on your hard disk This command is called the PATH command.

The PATH command lists specific drives and directories for DOS to search through when a command is issued. When you or one of your programs issues a command, DOS goes directly to the first drive/directory listed in the PATH statement. If the command is there, it executes it. If the command is not there, it moves to the second drive/directory in the PATH statement, and so on. If the proper drive/directory is not listed in the PATH statement, DOS gives you an error message to the effect that it can't find the file you're looking for, which means you have to type in the correct path as part of the command.

A typical path command looks something like this:

```
PATH C:\DOS;C:\;C:\WINDOWS;C:\EXCEL;C:\UTILITY;C:\DATA\EXCEL
```

Each directory is separated by a semicolon (;) and also includes the proper drive letter. Remember that DOS looks through the directories in the `PATH` statement in the order they appear. If you have similar commands/programs in multiple directories, put the one you want used at the head of the line!

Yikes!

You should include both your root directory (C:\) and your DOS directory in your `PATH` statement so DOS can find its own files!

One Extra Tip: Back Up Your Hard Disk!

One last thing about hard disks—*you need to be prepared for anything that can go wrong!* Because all your precious data resides on your hard disk, you're in really big trouble if anything happens to your disk. If your hard disk dies, all your data dies with it!

The best way to prepare for potential disaster is with a little insurance. The best insurance for hard disk disaster is a backup copy of all your important data. In fact, you should back up your hard disk on a regular basis—this way you're not too far behind if you have to access the backed-up data and restore it to your hard disk.

In versions of DOS prior to DOS 6, the DOS BACKUP command was used to back up data. The command looked something like this (if you were backing up all your files from drive C: to disks in drive A:):

```
BACKUP C:\*.* A: /S
```

With DOS 6 there is a new backup utility called Microsoft Backup that better automates the backup process. Microsoft Backup gives you a lot of backup options in a friendly utility program that uses pull-down menus instead of command-line switches.

Skip This, It's Technical!

Microsoft Backup in DOS 6 is available in both DOS and Windows versions. It's actually a limited version of Norton Backup, a very popular utility program from Symantec. You can use other backup programs, such as Central Point Backup and FastBack, which also automate the backup process.

To start Microsoft Backup, type the following at the DOS prompt:

```
MSBACKUP
```

PSST!

See your DOS 6 documentation for full instructions on using Microsoft Backup.

You'll need to set some options, but it's easy to do—and the results are worth it, especially if you ever need to restore lost data to your hard disk!

Index

Symbols

D

T

U

V

W

X–Y–Z

Book ISBN 0-672-30282-9